Phyllis Binkley

D0990466

Lou Gehrig

Pride of the Yankees

Courtesy of THE SPORTING NEWS

"Larruping Lou"—the Game's Iron Horse

LOU GEHRIG

Pride of the Yankees

by

PAUL GALLICO

With an Introduction by

BILL DICKEY

GROSSET & DUNLAP
Publishers   NEW YORK

Copyright, 1942, by
PAUL GALLICO

———

Foreword, Copyright, 1942, by
GROSSET & DUNLAP

Printed in the United States of America

CONTENTS

[v]

My Roommate Lou Gehrig

MY ROOMMATE LOU GEHRIG

by

Bill Dickey

PUTTING my memories of Lou Gehrig into words is a tough job. I'm supposed to be a baseball player, and sometimes I'm curious about calling myself that. But a writer is one thing I know I'm not.

For one thing it is impossible for me to realize that Lou, who was my roommate for years, is gone.

Lou's spirits never flinched. To me, he'll never be gone.

Lou and I hit it off perfectly from the first day I reported to the Yankees in 1928. I was a pretty green kid from the deep South, and just the idea of playing ball with the Yanks, who were the best team in baseball then (just as they are today) was enough to scare any rookie fresh from the minor leagues.

[3]

In the minors I had been a good hitter, very good, if I do say so myself. But the brand of pitching I had been facing was something different from the stuff the pitchers fed me in the American League. I couldn't seem to connect with a solid hit, and I couldn't figure out why.

The more I figured, and the more I worried about flopping with the Yanks, the worse my hitting got. Sometimes when I was at bat I noticed Lou studying me. I didn't know him so well then, although I was a great admirer of his long before I even came to the Yankees. He was four years older than I was, and was already famous by the time I joined the team.

Well, one day at batting practice he took me aside, and right then and there I really began to appreciate what a great guy Lou was.

"Listen, Bill," he said, "I have been watching you and I think I know what is wrong with your batting. Maybe I can help you correct it."

I was so pleased and surprised I could hardly answer. You see, in big league baseball, it is pretty much of a sink or swim business and big stars very seldom try to help a new kid improve himself. The competition is so keen that usually, as a matter of fact, the regulars kind of resent a promising rookie. He is supposed to find out how to improve himself, or get what help he needs from the manager or the coaches.

"You are trying to hit up at the ball, Bill," Lou went on. "These pitchers have too much stuff on the ball for you to get anywhere doing that. You might have some luck in the minors, with smaller parks and dumber pitchers, but up here you'll just hit flies to the outfield. Now, look and I'll show you what I mean."

And he worked with me for an hour or more, first showing me what I was doing, and explaining just why it was wrong, and then showing me the right way to do it. He did it every day for a few days, and pretty soon I began to catch on. I started to hit the ball, and except for a time after Lou got sick and I felt so blue I could hardly play ball at all, I've never had a serious batting slump since.

So you can see from that story alone why I thought so much of Lou. If he hadn't done that for me, the chances are that nobody else would have bothered, and maybe I'd have been a failure in the majors. Right now, instead of being pretty well fixed and as happy as a man can be in these times, I might have been kicking around in some tank town league, or maybe out of baseball altogether.

But then, as far as that's concerned, Lou was always doing something for rookies. Without even being asked he'd study their mistakes, and dope out just how to correct them, and he'd make the kid a better ball player in a few days.

"You're swinging ahead of the ball," he'd

say to some over-anxious youngster. Or he'd tip them off to the little mannerisms all pitchers have, little things that they do unconsciously that sometimes tip off a batter as to what kind of a pitch they're going to throw. I guess he was the best batting coach that ever lived.

And the remarkable part of this side of Lou is that nobody ever had to tell him much about hitting. It would have been easier to understand his interest in the rookies if he'd had a hard time learning himself.

Actually he was always such a good player that you might expect him to be impatient with other fellows who weren't so good. But not Lou. He always wanted to help other people. He was nice to everybody.

The way he treated the kids that used to swarm around him for autographs was even a pleasure. Sometimes, after you've just lost a tough game, it's annoying when kids stop you

[7]

as you leave the clubhouse. I've seen ball players, who were really swell fellows, brush right past some little fellow.

Once in a long time even Lou would be so upset when we'd dropped a game we needed badly that he'd ignore some child who wanted an autograph. He'd walk on a few steps, and then I'd hear him mumble to himself.

"Gee, wait a minute, it wasn't that kid's fault that we got licked."

And he'd walk back.

"Come here, Sonny, I guess I didn't see you before." And to be extra considerate, he'd stop and chat with the lad for a few minutes.

Everybody knows that on the field Lou was one of the smartest ball players who ever lived. But I don't think people realize how intelligent he was about other things, particularly world affairs.

As far back as 1935 or '36, Lou would tell me that the whole world was going to be at war soon. He'd complain that we ought to start preparing for it. Sometimes the other players would kid him about it, and tell him nothing could ever happen to the United States, and that we'd never have to go to war again. I guess I did, too. But Lou foresaw the war pretty accurately.

The thing that made him madder than anything else were the German-American Bunds. He'd see pictures of a big Bund meeting in the newspaper, and he would turn to me and say:

"Bill, I would like to go up there with a baseball bat and break up one of those little get-togethers all by myself. I would smack some of those skulls a lot harder than I ever hit a baseball."

He felt very keenly because it was Germany that seemed to be responsible for all the danger even then, and being of German stock, this affected him very deeply.

"When they come over here and settle," he'd say of those Germans in the Bunds, "they become Americans. It's a disgrace for them to act like that. I wish they would take them all out to the desert in planes and drop them out without parachutes."

Yes, Lou was of German descent; but he was less like a Nazi than anyone you can imagine. Between seasons I love to go hunting, and many times I tried to get Lou to come along with me. He refused because he couldn't bear the thought of killing anything, even an animal.

Peculiarly, I remember one time he explained this to me—almost as though he were saying it now.

"When I was a kid I went out bird shooting with some friends," he told me, after I'd invited him to go on a deer hunting trip with me down south. "I shot a bird, and do you know, Bill, after I saw it, lying on the ground dead, I felt so badly I cried. I dug a grave for it and buried it there, and I swore I'd never go hunting again."

He liked fishing though, and we fished a lot,

all up and down the Atlantic Coast. But what do you think he would do, once he'd landed a big one after a hard fight? He'd loosen the hook, and throw it back in the ocean. He was the only man I ever knew about whom you could really say that he wouldn't harm a living thing—except those boys in the Bund.

He was such a good sport that one of his favorite sports was fishing for big ocean fish with light fresh water tackle. I've seen him battle a big kingfish for half an hour with a little bass rod, and then throw it back when he had landed it.

As a roommate, he was practically perfect. He was the neatest, most methodical man I ever knew. With him everything had to be in its proper place. I'm ashamed to say that I'm almost the opposite, so Lou would have to go around picking up after me.

"Listen, you big dumbbell, you'd leave your head around some place if I wasn't here to watch out for you," he would shout at me, sometimes, after I'd forgotten something, a necktie, say, when we went from one hotel to another on a road trip. I'd lay for him, and try to find something that he'd forgotten when we were traveling, but he was too smart and I never succeeded.

One of the things I admired most in Lou was the way he overcame his shyness. When I first knew him, even though he was quite famous by that time, he was the shyest man I ever knew. Often some of the fellows on the team would be asked to attend some banquet or some function that was really important.

"I'll go on one condition," Lou would always say, "that I don't have to do anything or say anything. I'd rather get beaned with a fast ball than have to get up and make a speech."

But all of a sudden, about five or six years ago, he blossomed out into a grand speaker. He'd get up at any occasion without the least bit of embarrassment—and make a fine talk.

Sometimes he would discuss baseball, but toward the last, when the war was coming closer and closer, you could not get him to talk about anything but the defense of democracy.

One night in Madison Square Garden he made a short speech at a big banquet. He talked about tolerance. He brought down the house. I think it was his wife, Eleanor, a really wonderful woman, who helped him overcome that painful early embarrassment in front of strangers.

As well as I knew Lou during those happy years when he was probably the healthiest, strongest man alive, I don't think I really got to know what an absolutely wonderful human being he was until he started to get sick.

From the time he reported at the training camp in St. Petersburg in the spring of 1939, there was something wrong with him, but of course neither he nor anyone else had any idea it was serious. At first, when he didn't come around into shape quickly, the way he used to (he always kept himself in shape, for that matter), he would kid about it.

"Well, the old Iron Horse is only human after all, I'm afraid," he'd say. "I guess I'm getting old."

And then he would work himself unbelievably, to the limit of his endurance, to overcome what he thought was the usual stiffening up that comes to all athletes getting along in years.

He would go out early in the morning and run until those powerful legs of his couldn't take another step. Then he would force himself through the regular workout with the team.

When we came home after the practice, he would spend an hour or so doing all kinds of strenuous bending exercises. But the more he worked, the worse he became. He would stumble on the field making some easy play, for days he couldn't get a hit against the minor leaguers we played on the trip north.

Lou had always been a very even-tempered

fellow, easy and pleasant, but coming north that year he got very moody. He would sit in the room and say nothing at all for a long time. When I'd try to cheer him up and tell him I thought he was coming around at last, he would hardly even answer me.

By that time, having been around him so long and knowing his little habits and peculiarities so well, I was beginning to realize that there was something the matter with him. Something that had nothing to do with him getting older. After all he was only thirty-five and he had always taken perfect care of himself.

Then one day something happened in the room that convinced me. He started to take a little step forward to get something, and the foot he moved forward to start the step just didn't move right. Instead of swinging right out, it just moved a few inches in a faltering kind of way, and it threw Lou off balance, and he stumbled to the floor.

He looked up with a shocked and embarrassed expression. I knew it was no time for clowning. I felt then that it was something terrible happening.

A few days later the same thing happened in the dressing-room. He took a real bad fall as he started to undress, and the boys did the same as I did. Nobody wanted to humiliate him by going to his aid, and he dragged himself off the floor, looking sort of dazed, as if somebody had struck him down from behind.

That day in Detroit, when he asked Joe McCarthy to take him off first and put in Babe Dahlgren, was a day none of us who were there will ever forget. Lou came walking into the dugout, dragging his feet and with his head down low, and all the boys, just as if they had made some sort of agreement beforehand, went on with the game as if nothing had happened.

We knew it would only make things worse if we tried to cheer him up. Right after that he went out to the Mayo Clinic, and soon we found out that his playing days were over.

It was after he came back he showed his real class. He must have known the disease had him licked, but he wouldn't admit it. I think he was just trying to keep up a pretense because he didn't want his wife and his pals to feel badly. The last time I saw him, just before he died, he even went to great lengths to explain to me that the doctors had told him he was reaching the turning point in his sickness.

"I'll be all right, Bill," he said. "The doctors tell me that I have to get down very low, and that then my body will start fighting those germs and I'll start to improve. I'll be out there playing next year, showing those youngsters how first base ought to be played."

Hundreds of people who didn't know Lou, except to read about him and see him play, have asked me the same question about him:

"Lou Gehrig seems to have been a man without a real weakness, without even a fault. Is it true, Bill? Could there be such a man?"

[17]

Well, there was. I suppose I knew Lou better than any man alive, and to me he will always be the greatest guy that ever lived. He was all man, in every meaning of the word, physically, mentally, morally and spiritually. I'll never meet another guy like him.

Lou Gehrig

Pride of the Yankees

1

THE TIME, THE PLACE—AND THE MAN

OUT by the flagpole in center field of the Yankee Stadium, the ball park which during the glittering Golden Decade was the home of the greatest slugging team that baseball has ever known, there stands today a newly erected bronze plaque.

Raised on it in relief, is the bust of a man wearing a baseball cap and uniform. And the inscription thereon reads—

"Henry Louis Gehrig. June 19, 1903=June 2, 1941. A man, a gentleman, and a great ball player, whose amazing record of 2,130 consecutive games should stand for all time. This memorial is a tribute from the Yankee players to their beloved captain and teammate, July 4, 1941."

LOU GEHRIG

Of all the great and glamorous athletes, the gigantic and sometimes screwy sports figures of the Dizzy Decade, who clattered across the sports stage with fuss and fume and fury, and the thunder and lightning of their compelling personalities, Lou Gehrig, the ball player, was probably the simplest, the most retiring, the most sensitive and honest.

During the greater part of his playing career, he was completely overshadowed by the gigantic, eye and publicity compelling figure of George Herman Ruth, the Babe.

It was an era of giants into which he was born, figures so arresting and well publicized that it seemed necessary to name but one or two to represent each of the great sports.

When you had said Babe Ruth in baseball, Tunney and Dempsey in boxing, Bill Tilden and Helen Wills in tennis, Bob Jones in golf, Paddock and Nurmi on the running tracks, Earl Sande the jockey, Knute Rockne and Red Grange on the gridiron and Tommy

Hitchcock on the polo field, there was a swift and comprehensive statement of the era.

But along with these, were many hundreds of great athletes, men and women, colorful and capable, but whose efforts were overshadowed by the individual brilliance of the leaders.

One of these was Lou Gehrig, Yankee first baseman, iron man, slugger and team captain, who batted in fourth position after Babe Ruth on Murderer's Row.

Life itself, or Fate or Circumstance, call it what you will, made of the late Lou Gehrig one of the most dramatic, tragic and gallant figures ever to stride across the American sports scene, a scene which has been so great a part of our national life.

He was described as a plain, humdrum fellow with not much color.

He never considered himself either unusual or outstanding.

It was the American public with its close

to infallible sound, common sense and simple good judgment that made of Lou Gehrig a national hero.

Because, what happened to Lou Gehrig, his life, his struggles, his one love, and his ending, far transcends that evanescent, glittery, surface stuff called color. In interest, and in the tug upon the heartstrings, it outweighs sports and the figures of sport. Lou Gehrig went far beyond the newsprint accolade of being listed as one of the great athletes of the first quarter of the century, and even beyond being named, as he was, by experts and veterans of the game, as the greatest first baseman that ever lived.

He entered the hearts of the American people, because of his living as well as his passing, he became and was to the end, a great and splendid human being.

And so I am calling this brief biographical sketch—"Lou Gehrig—An American Hero," because he was a hero and because he was wholly our own.

He was not an American bred to the soil of many generations of Anglo-Saxon blood, but first generation.

His parents were Germans. He was born three years after they immigrated to America, at the turn of the century. But he was an American in body and soul, through that great and blessed spirit that vitalizes this country and that leaps like lightning through the veins of the newborn of this land, no matter what their background, or bloodstreams. Everything that Henry Louis Gehrig did from the day that he could walk and talk, until his ending, was as American as Bunker Hill, Valley Forge, the Rocky Mountains, or the Dakota Prairies.

His is an American story, a boy of foreign born parents who rose from poverty to dignity and success, and his virtues are the virtues that are admired by American people and which in the past have helped to guide us.

He was a naive man, but then we are also a naive people. In every way, but in particular in the details of his brave and gallant end, he lived the kind of life that we know is good, a life that we have come to believe, and with considerable cause, is something that is our own, and in a way, indigenous to this country.

The kind of a man Lou Gehrig was would have been neither liked nor admired in Germany. He would not have been understood in France, or appreciated in England. Nor would the Europe of today understand why we Americans feel about him the way we do, why we write his biography, why we are preparing to screen the life of a man who was neither statesman, politician, national patriot or soldier, who was merely a paid performer, a professional athlete, an entertainer, whose existence did not so much as by the millionth part of the weight of a hair, tip the balance of history.

There was once a country in Europe that would have understood, and which in its own way perpetuated the name and fame of men who were like Gehrig, a country in which the slogan—"In mens sano, corpore sano," a clean mind in a healthy body, was a living thing. The Golden Age of Greece knew how to admire the simple virtues too, a Greece that two thousand years ago was a Democracy.

What will you say of Lou Gehrig beyond that he lived a good and useful life, set a fine example to others and was cut off by tragic mischance at the height of his career?

But somehow, it is only we the naive and the simple here in America who understand and feel how much we today stand in the need of stories like that of Lou Gehrig, tales of honest, trustworthy men, born on our own soil, life patterns that are not crossed by blackness,

[27]

or chicanery, vice, or intrigue, careers that are not poisoned by double dealing, jealousy or opportunism, love stories that are simple and virtuous and true. We need them to get back our own faith in the values of simple and decent living.

It is good and sweet and comforting to write about a poor boy who conquered life's handicaps, about a young athlete who was proud of his skill and took care of his body, about a shy young lover who suffered because he felt he was unworthy of the girl he had learned to love, and who when he won her, was loyal, faithful, kind and grateful to the end for the love that had come to him. And it is inspiring to tell the story of a man who gave value and more, penny for penny, for what he was paid, who gave of his strength unsparingly and unstintingly, with never a thought for himself, and who in the end, knew for over a year that he must die of a hopeless malady, but who had no thought but to keep the knowledge from his wife, and who did no single thing that was not brave and gallant, to his last breath.

The American people, I think, did themselves much honor when they named Gehrig "hero" and from their hearts tendered him his final ovations. For in the end, we will strive to be like that which we admire. We are a truly unique nation in the simple qualities of our ethics. Gehrig is a hero drawn from our national life and our national concept of the living of life. What have we to do in thought or concept with those people who name as their heroes, boys who press bomb release levers over crowded cities to spatter human flesh blindly and wilfully?

Henry Louis Gehrig was only a few days short of thirty-eight when he died, but he spanned in that lifetime, almost a complete cycle of history, and certainly, two of the greatest sports eras America has ever known— pre and post World War I. The men who were the great baseball stars of his boyhood were the fading players of his early days in the game. And the country into which he had been born a citizen was preparing to go to war against the country his parents had left behind them.

2

YOUTH OF A HERO

TURN the clock back to the summer and fall of 1915, and the effect is curious. Britain was warning Bulgaria, saying that Germany sought to disrupt the Balkans and enslave the states that played her game. President Wilson was snarling at the German submarine warfare, and Congress was to be asked for $400,000,000 to begin national defense, and raise the Army to 120,000 men. William Gillette was playing a return engagement of Sherlock Holmes, and the Boston Red Sox beat the Phillies in the World Series by five games to one.

On the Boston team was an outfielder named Tris Speaker, a little shortstop named Everett Scott, and a new pitcher come up from Baltimore only the year before called Babe Ruth. And the great pitching star of that season and who the Phillies counted upon—in vain—to win the world series for them, was Grover Cleveland Alexander.

Lou Gehrig at that time was twelve years old, a shy, worried, harassed youngster in cast-off clothes, attending P. S. 132 in Manhattan, and living on upper Amstredam Avenue where he was known as the Heini janitor's kid.

It was ten years before Murderer's row and the glamorous sports figures of the Golden Decade, but there were great names in baseball to fascinate a little boy who loved the game and was trying in an awkward, left handed way to play it.

Ty Cobb led the American League in batting for the ninth consecutive year, Walter Johnson was burning them over the plate for the Washington Senators, and on July 4th, a boy named George Sisler, a former University of Michigan baseball star pitched for the

Browns of St. Louis, and won his game 3 to 1.

The New York Giants had Snodgrass and Burns and Fletcher, and Fred Merkle of boner fame, Hans Lobert and Chief Myers and Larry Doyle. Rube Marquart and Jeff Tesreau and Christy Mathewson pitched for them.

Heine Zimmerman, Zack Wheat and Jake Daubert were names to conjure with on the Brooklyn club. And on the not particularly distinguished team of the New York Yankees for that year, along with Andy High and Roger Peckinpaugh and a heterogeneous assortment of athletes, was a tall stringbean of a first baseman by the name of Wally Pipp. "Pipp the Pickler," the sports writers dubbed him, because he was a handy fellow with the ash and had been known to break up many a ball game with a well placed hit.

These were the famous names of the day, and these were the heroes of young Looie Gehrig, the Janitor's kid, who in a clumsy left handed way was trying to play baseball himself, and dreaming his dreams. He knew them all by name and sight, he had their likenesses on the wonderful souvenir picture cards that came with the Sweet Caporal cigarettes his old man smoked, or in certain types of penny candy which he got as an occasional treat.

Like all boys of that age, he traded busily in these pictures and he tried to play ball with the kids around the lot and the school team. He was not particularly welcome around the pick-up games, because after all what could anyone do with a left handed catcher—right handed catcher's mitts were hard enough to come by—and a weak and timid hitter who shied away from the plate? AND a Dutchman to boot! Damn those Henies! They were torturing babies in Belgium. The papers said so.

But the boy was not war conscious then and those things were not yet his concern. He

cared more about the things he read in the
papers of the doings of the bright stars of the
baseball world, and talking them over with his
schoolmates.

But imaginative as boys are in erecting their
marvelous castles in the sky, could the boy
Gehrig ever in his wildest flight of fancy have
seen himself in a Yankee uniform invading the
Detroit dugout and taking a swing at the famous Ty Cobb for riding him? Or batting
against the great Alexander in a World
Series? Or breaking the consecutive games
record of that same Everett Scott who played
for the Red Sox that year?

Could he imagine that some day Miller
Huggins, manager of the New York Yankees
would say—"Gehrig—get out there on First
Base. You're taking Pipp's place"?

Surely he might have hoped some day to
play big league ball, as all kids yearn for fame
and fortune. But not even in his dizziest day
dream could he have imagined himself hitting

in fourth position behind a man who was to become known as the greatest home run hitter the world has ever seen, or foresee that in the end he would become a better player and a greater figure than that same man, Babe Ruth, and be judged by experts to have been the greatest first baseman the game had ever known, rated even above the superb Frank Chance.

Yet all of these things were to happen to the husky, slow-footed kid who was getting his early schooling on the hard, rough sidewalks of New York.

Henry Louis Gehrig was born at 179th Street and Amsterdam Avenue, Manhattan, on June 19th, 1903. His parents, Henry and Christina Gehrig were German immigrants who had come to America at the beginning of the century. Henry Gehrig was an artisan, an iron worker, that is, he made ornamental grilles for doors and railings and balustrades —when he could get work at his trade. And when he didn't, he got what work he could, odd jobs and whatnot until he landed a steady job as a janitor.

Mrs. Gehrig was a solid German hausfrau who knew her place and duty in life. That place was the kitchen, the duty to feed and look after her family.

They were strangers in a strange land. America does miracles for the first generation born here. Youngsters of north, or central, or southern European blood seem literally to be born with a liberty bell in one hand a fielder's mitt on the other.

But the old folks who emigrated here did not assimilate as quickly. They clung to the old ways and the old ideas. Much of what went on in this new and teeming land they did not understand, or even attempt to understand, though they recognized the opportunities.

The Gehrigs were decent, sober, uninspired folk who brought up their surviving son in the strict, old-fashioned way. There had been other children who had died, either at birth, or very soon after. Little Looie was a sickly child for a spell too, but somehow the air of the new country finally managed to get into his lungs and swell him out and filled him up, and the wholesome cooking of Mama Gehrig did the rest. Like so many first generation American kids born of foreign parents, he grew to astonishing proportions.

His early home life was European in the sense that there was less affection for Lou than is usual in, let us say, a typical American home. In the German home, the father is king and master, and amongst the poorer people who are engaged in a constant struggle for existence there is even less time for the sentimental relationship between parents and child that marks our modern American families. Henry Louis was no stranger to corporal punishment at the hands of his father.

Early in life he became imbued with a sense of his own worthlessness which he never overcame to the end of his days. He just never understood how he could possibly be any good, or how anybody could really love or care for him. When he married, he used to break his wife's heart with the constant reproaches he cast at himself. Her most difficult task was to build in him some slight approximation of his true worth so that others would not go on taking advantage of him.

As a man, his greatest handicap was that he was super-sensitive, shy, self-accusing, quick to take hurt and slow to recover therefrom.

His boyhood was responsible for this. So was the twig bent. He was a big boy for his age, big and slow witted. Smaller kids would gang up and chase him. They called him "chicken heart," with that refined cruelty of gamin children, threw stones at him, chased him away from their games, wouldn't let him play ball with them, hooted his ineptness at things that came naturally to them, such as running and swimming, and hitting a ball with a stick.

At first this was the normal trial of any kid

on any block who is awkward and oversized and has not yet found himself. Eventually, he gained some sort of tolerance, swam with them off the old Coal Barge in the Harlem River near the Old High Bridge, got chased by cops and was once even arrested for swimming without trunks. There was a fine scandal in the Gehrig household when Pop had to come down to the police station and bring him home. Their boy in jail already. A bummer he was becoming with them good-for-nothing loafers. Looie got a good smacking.

But later, when he was fourteen, the war came and the inevitable witch hunts spread even to his neighborhood. His old folks were Germans, and Germans were enemies. That terrible time too had its effect on the character of the boy. Added to his poverty and awkwardness, it drove him still further away from his own kind, pitched him still lower in his own estimation.

There was nothing at which he was very good, neither studies, nor the game of baseball which he had grown to love and which he longed to master. He was an undistinguished fifth wheel on the P. S. 132 ball team, a left handed catcher who couldn't hit the length of his cap, a chicken heart who was so ball shy at the plate that even when he reached college he had to be cured of batting with one foot practically in the dugout.

But no matter what the atmosphere or the fortunes of the Gehrig home, the handicaps of poverty and a low scale of living, one thing must not be forgotten, and Lou Gehrig never forgot it. His mother was insistent that he avail himself of the great opportunity provided by this new land in which they were living . . . education. Poor they might be, and insignificant in the social scale, but her Looie had the same opportunity to become educated as the richest boy in the land.

And so when Gehrig graduated from P. S. 132, instead of being sent out to find work to augment the meager family budget, he was urged to continue school, and entered New

York's famous High School of Commerce at 66th Street and 10th Avenue.

What Gehrig's education was like in those years, I know from experience because I was just four years ahead of him through the same mill. My parents had emigrated from Europe in 1897. While Gehrig was attending P. S. 132, I was at P. S. 6. When Gehrig entered Commerce High School, I was just finishing at De Witt Clinton High School, Commerce's great rival. And when Lou entered Columbia University, I had just finished working my way through the same institution.

And no one knows better than I the deep love for America that was in the heart of Lou Gehrig, or the boundless gratitude to the country that made caste, race, creed or poverty no bar and provided equal opportunity for all.

Commerce was a long distance away from upper Amsterdam Avenue, but his parents provided him with carfare, or he walked, or hitched on delivery wagons as all kids did in those days, and they could always provide him with a lunch box, and a nickel to get a bottle of milk in the General Organization lunch room.

Glimpses of Gehrig in high school may be culled from letters written to me by men who were his schoolmates in high school.

Arthur Allen Narins writers from Philadelphia—"No one who went to school with Lou can forget the cold winter days and Lou coming to school wearing khaki shirt, khaki pants and heavy brown shoes, but no overcoat, nor any hat. He was a poor boy."

Incidentally, that hardening that Gehrig got as a youngster became a lifetime habit. He never wore a hat, vest or overcoat in the coldest weather until after his marriage when his wife, frantic at his flirting with pneumonia, finally managed to get him into a winter overcoat.

The rebuffs that Gehrig had suffered as a boy when he had tried to play with the kids on the block already had their effect upon him when he went to high school. Oliver Gintel, now a prosperous furrier in New York, writes:

"In my first year at Commerce, I was trying to get a berth on the Soccer team. In practice one day, I kicked the ball accidentally towards a huskily built boy (Lou) who booted the thing nonchalantly across almost the entire length of the practice field.

"I approached him to try out for the team. He refused, stating that he wasn't good at athletics, and besides, his mother wouldn't give him permission.

"I arranged for Doc Reynolds, our coach, to watch this boy kick a ball and he repeated his performance. But he turned Reynolds down. Lou was being criticized for his utter lack of school spirit, and was being called a sissy and a mama's boy. Always smiling, he paid no attention to any criticism and minded his own business. I then went to work on him in earnest for a week. He eventually did make the team, played for three seasons as half-back. He won the winter championship for three successive years while he was a member of the team."

3

THE MAKING OF AN ATHLETE

APPARENTLY, Lou had managed to convert his parents to the importance of sport in the life of an American boy, something that Europeans would find hard to understand, for he also played on the football team, and returned to his first love in sports, baseball.

He was ordered to report for baseball practice, and turned up in his street clothes and shoes to drill with the team, for he didn't own so much as a pair of spikes, or a glove. Eventually he was given a uniform. But the curious thing was that whereas he was a brilliant soccer player and a capable prospect on the football field, he was a poor performer on the diamond.

He was made a first baseman, because the

team was in need of another infielder, and in his first year batted only .150.

But here entered two factors that were to follow him through life. The first was his own dogged persistence and his desire to learn and improve himself, and the second was the faith in him that somehow, in spite of his clumsiness and awkwardness, he inspired in the men who taught the game.

Harry Kane, coach of the Commerce baseball team was the first of these, and Gehrig always gave him full credit for correcting his early faults as a hitter. Day after day, Kane would take the boy and pitch to him for fifteen minute stretches. The next year he was already hitting .300.

Those high school years were important to Gehrig. Things happened to him and to his family that were to have a powerful influence on his future.

For one thing, a crisis overtook the family, one that threatened to bring his education to an end. His father became stricken with some form of paralysis, temporarily, and was no longer able to work. The meagre Gehrig exchequer dwindled away to nothing. To the rescue came both Mama Gehrig and Lou.

They were strong, brave, determined people, these old country mothers. No matter what their failings, they could take a blow, and strike back. She went to work, answered an advertisement for a cook and housekeeper for the Phi Delta Theta fraternity house at Columbia University, took in washing on the side, scrimped, saved, worried, nursed her husband and somehow kept her own kitchen going. She was determined that Lou should continue with his schooling.

Young Lou went to work too, after school hours. He got jobs in butcher shops and grocery stores, running errands, minding kids, delivering papers, any one of the many ways a kid around New York those days could earn a few dollars a week.

And somehow he was managing to attend baseball practice for the school team as well. It is difficult to realize unless you have been through it, what a fantastic amount of study, work and play can be got in by a kid with a fair constitution and a willingness to be on the go from dawn to midnight. Sometimes I used to talk to other chaps working their way through school, and we agreed that if we should have to sweat as hard in after life as we were then, there wasn't much to look forward to.

That was the training that Gehrig had.

Summer vacations meant steadier work and a little reserve added to the Gehrig bank account. And it also meant that Gehrig on Sundays could pick up ball games around his neighborhood at places like Reservoir Oval and Bennett Field. Those were the famous sandlot games out of which came some pretty fair ball players, though none as famous as Gehrig eventually became.

He even appeared in a uniform with a petty

semi-pro outfit called the Minqua Baseball Club sponsored by the Assembly district Democratic Club of that name at West 181st Street. They played mostly little semi-pro clubs from New Jersey, and also neighboring Democratic districts.

And it wasn't idling. The clubs played for $35 guarantees. Of this the battery mates got $5.00 each. Here Lou abandoned first base where the increment was low and became a pitcher. That $5.00 every Sunday was important money.

Such was life around New York for a poor boy. You will find it paralleled by thousands upon thousands of youngsters in similar circumstances. In many ways it was an exciting and engrossing life, this battle against the world's greatest city, for education, sustenance and joy. And it too had an important bearing on Gehrig's character, his make-up and behavior in later life. It imposed upon him virtues that he never lost.

Gehrig in later years was sometimes snickered at as a paragon of virtues. He didn't drink or wench, or stay up in night clubs, or get involved in scandals. He kept in rigid training and was always in top condition, his pleasures were simple, he smoked only mildly, he was good to his mother and faithful to his wife.

Home training had much to do with this, besides the sound soul and spirit of the boy, but the early habits of his life were also greatly responsible. The matter of time takes on a great importance; time, and the games he learned to love to play.

Even if a boy is basically sound, there is plenty of trouble for him to get into around New York, especially if he lives in a poor neighborhood, where the kids tend to drift into bands, or young gangs, groups that start as a rivalry to the bunch down the next block, and which can easily drift into pilfering, window smashing and other petty offences which later lead to the higher brackets of misdemeanor and crime.

But there are just so many hours to a waking day, and if every minute of them is occupied bread-winning, attending school, or playing on some kind of team, there is simply no time left for mischief.

Physical condition is a part of the American system of competition and free enterprise. The regimens whereby it is achieved are strictly self imposed. It is acquired in direct proportion to the ambition of the boy who cares to practice it.

The bright and desirable prizes are held out to the youngster—a place on the team, a uniform, a letter, a trip. The coach makes the simple rules of training and points out what kind of an athlete is wanted on the team. And the ambition of the individual does the rest.

Gehrig's clean living did not grow out of a smugness and prudery, a desire for personal sanctification. He had a stubborn, pushing ambition. He wanted something. He chose the most sensible and efficient route to getting it. Since control of his body was an important factor in his desire to excel in those sports in which he took part, he took care of it in an intelligent manner. Hundreds of thousands of boys in America are doing the same thing all over the country today.

Habits formed in youth are apt to last through later life. Gehrig's did. He never made a parade of his virtues, or even considered them as such. He merely lived the way he liked to live.

Once he even went on a two weeks bender. It is one of my favorite stories, because somehow more than anything it has the tender quality of the naive simplicity of the guy. To his wife, though it happened long before they met, it is known lovingly as Lou's two weeks' drunk.

It occurred when he was a raw young rookie but recently signed with the Yankees and farmed out by them for seasoning to the Minor League Hartford Club of the Eastern League.

Midway in the season the boy fell into an

awful batting slump. Day after day went by
without his getting a hit. He saw his cherished career ending before it had begun. He
was certain he would be cast off to some class
C club.

One night he went out with some of the boys
on the team and they all wound up in a speak-
easy drinking a lot of early prohibition gin.
And since nothing seemed to matter any more,
and life was over, Gehrig drank too.

He drank an awful lot of gin and got roar-
ing tight and the next morning felt like the
cold clinkers of hell, with a head on him
like a Gordon Bennett balloon. Somehow he
dragged himself out to the ball yard, into his
monkey suit and up to the plate.

Thereupon the great miracle took place.
Aching, foggy, half-sick, he proceeded to tear
the cover off the ball. Home runs, doubles,
triples rattled off his bat.

He even fielded his position with an ele-
gance and ease he had never known before,

having been named the world's clumsiest first baseman at the outset of his career.

That night he went out and bought a quart of gin, imbibed it dutifully and without much pleasure, since it tasted horrible and made his mouth feel like the inside of a second baseman's glove the next morning, but the results were apparent to anyone sitting in the ball park or looking at the box score, and the opposing pitchers in the end suffered more than Gehrig did.

To make assurance doubly sure, he took to transferring potions of the life-giving fluid into little medicine bottles and carrying them in his uniform, and he would sneak nips in the dugout while awaiting his turn at bat. He was never sober for a moment.

Finally, at the end of two weeks, Pat O'Conner, the manager of the Hartford team, caught on and called in his big, awkward slugger for a little fatherly talk. O'Conner had gone to a lot of trouble developing him into the hitter he had become and he wasn't going to see him turn into a baseball bum like some of the others.

He said gruffly, but not unkindly—"What the Hell is going on here, Lou? I never knew you to take a drink before. Don't you know those guys you're going with are all wrong for you? They're just a lotta guys on their way out. You're headin' to be like them before you've got started. Maybe you're just a big, dumb Dutchman, but I think you've got a chance to go places in baseball, or I wouldn't be wasting my time here talking to you. But you'll never be a star, drunk all the time and carrying on and carousing with a bunch of bums. Get it?"

The most surprised man in the world was Henry Louis Gehrig. He turned baffled and horror stricken blue eyes on O'Conner.

"Drinking and carousing! I wasn't doing that, Pat. Why looka how I been hitting the last two weeks. It's wonderful. And two

weeks ago I couldn't lift a fly out of the infield. I just came on it by accident."

O'Conner was a wise old gentleman. He
didn't laugh. He explained carefully, pa-
tiently and thoroughly the effects of alcohol
on athletes, its habit forming proclivities, and
what it would do to him eventually if he kept
it up.

And that was the end of Lou Gehrig's hitting medicine, and his two weeks' spree. He
drank beer in later life, but kept away from
spirits. And he kept away from them not because of any prissy notions of righteousness
that it was evil or wrong to take a drink but
because he had a driving, non-stop ambition
to become a great and successful ball player.
Anything that interfered with that ambition
was poison to him.

4

"THERE WAS A MAN NAMED RUTH"

THE high school period continues interesting. For in his final year at Commerce, Gehrig caught his first real glimpses of that other and more luxurious world away from Tenth and Amsterdam Avenues into which he was soon to move.

For one thing, he took a part time job as a waiter in the Phi Delta Theta house, the famous aristocratic Fiddle-de-thates of Columbia University, just off the campus, where his mother was cooking and housekeeping.

And for another he took his first trip away from home, pullman, first class best hotel, all expenses, when that recently-born tabloid, the Daily News, sent the championship Commerce baseball team out to Chicago to play an inter-city game with Lane Tech High, winners of the Chicago title.

The New York boys beat the Chicago boys by the score of 12 to 6. Lou Gehrig the first baseman didn't get a hit in three times at bat, but the fourth time he appeared at the platter the bases were full and Gehrig poled one over the right field wall, out of the park and down the street. It was an adult wallop that any major league ball player would have been glad to have hit.

It was a red blooded robust clout. And as the result of it, for the first time the shadow of another man, a Great Personage fell athwart the kid player. A reformed pitcher had come to the New York Yankees from the Boston Red Rox, and was piling up a prodigious amount of home runs for them. His name of course was Babe Ruth.

And they called Lou Gehrig the "Babe Ruth of the High Schools."

In Gehrig's own scrap book with the name

"LOU GEHRIG" printed on the outside in gold letters, there is on the first page an already yellowing clipping of a photograph of the President of the Board of Education congratulating the victorious team, and there is prominently displayed a sign—"OH YOU BABE RUTH," while another says "HAIL TO THE VICTORS!"

Babe Ruth! Lou Gehrig! Two names that were to be coupled for so long. And always Babe Ruth first and Lou Gehrig after. Strange that even his first day of glory he shared with the Babe and was named under his great shadow. Strange, that is, now that we can see his career as a whole and realize how long Lou Gehrig played in the shadow of Ruth in every way, how long it was before he came into his own, and how tragically short his glory was then.

But the big Dutchman from upper Amsterdam Avenue was probably quite delighted with the honor done to him. To be called a

"Babe Ruth" was better even than being called conqueror, or mayor, or president.

Mama and Papa Gehrig did not quite know what the fuss was all about, or who this *"Baby Root"* was, but it was nice their boy Looie's picture was in the paper, along with a write-up, only now it shouldn't go to his head so he should become a bummer like some of them other kids what used to be on the block, but he should work hard and study and maybe he could go inside Columbia and be a *"Collision"* which was Mama Gehrig's version of a collegian.

It should be added here that neither Mama nor Papa had ever seen a baseball game or had any idea what *that* was about except that it seemed to amuse Looie and keep him off the street, and sometimes when he got older he brought five dollars home from it, not from gambling, but what he got paid.

But what Mama Gehrig did know through her labors at the fraternity house was that *col-*

litsch was a fine place, and *collisions* were fine boys and that in this amazing country her boy could be a *collision* too and carry books and later have a fine job or profession, whereas in her country they would have tossed him into the Army when he came of age and the Prussian Junkerdom wouldn't have let him come near a university.

Lou Gehrig graduated from Commerce and in 1922 matriculated at Columbia University, aided by a scholarship awarded him not for what lay between his ears but because he was 210 pounds of bone and muscle and was willing to give on the field of sport.

About this time you will find in his scrap book mysterious clippings referring to one "Lou Long," a husky left-handed hitter and first baseman who played in the Oranges and around Newark with the Westinghouse semi-pro team, and again a newspaper notice of a certain first baseman, Gerry of the Yonkers team, who lifted one over the scoreboard at the West New York playground, with two aboard in one of the longest hits ever seen on that field.

It was just little Looie doing his best to help out Mom, the summer of 1922 before turning up at Columbia.

But it should be here noted and recorded that for all his clippings, for all his semi-pro earnings and for all of being called "The Babe Ruth of This," and "The Babe Ruth of That," Henry Louis Gehrig had no idea of a career as a major league ball player when he entered Columbia University, because he signed up for the pre-engineering course. He wanted to become an engineer. Why, he did not know exactly, but he later told his wife Eleanor that he kind of liked the picture of himself in riding pants and leather boots, shirt open at the neck and wide brimmed hat, reading from a blue print out West and telling the boys where to put the dam.

At Columbia, Gehrig had the finishing

touches applied to him that resulted in his becoming completely girl-shy and frightened of the female of the species from then on until he met the only woman he ever loved or wholly trusted, the girl that he married.

And the same experience likewise tended to withdraw him even more within himself, and to fill him with a sense of his own unworthiness and lack of everything.

Arrived on the Columbia campus and immediately a football star, Lou Gehrig was made a member of the fraternity wherein his mother was working as a cook, and where he himself worked as a waiter to help earn his college keep.

This on the face of it would seem to be a diamond studded example of the workings of our Democracy, except that in truth and fairness to justice, it didn't quite work out that way.

Actually it was Gehrig who honored the Fiddle-de-thates by joining up, rather than the other way around. In those days, fraternity rushing at Columbia was a fiercely contested affair fraught with considerable jealousy and backbiting, and freshmen who looked as though they might someday become star athletes and shed their light upon their brothers, were plums, and Lou Gehrig was a plum de luxe. They took him in, not because they wanted to, but because they had to. If they hadn't, another fraternity would have.

But Gehrig reported in later life that they weren't very nice to him. He was a brother all right, but he wasn't quite as much of a brother as some of the other lads whose mothers weren't cooks. The boys managed somehow to convey that fine distinction to him. It was the first time that the big, rough, dumb Dutchman butted into the wall reared by the so-called upper classes. It bled a little where he hit, and left a scar. In fact, the brothers never did warm up to him until he became the famous Yankee first baseman and heir to the throne of Babe Ruth. Then they would come around and give him the grip and remember the good old days in the frat house and how jolly it all was. And Gehrig's lip would curl, because he was remembering other things.

For instance, how, many a night after he had helped his mother clean up the kitchen, had washed the dishes, and studied, he would sleep in his clothes in a chair in the fraternity house, too tired out to go home. Also because he had to be on the spot early in the morning to help his mother get breakfast for the boys.

And he was probably remembering the humiliations and heartaches that came with wearing clothes that always had a patch in them somewhere, of being in the college and playing for the college, but never actually being *of* the college.

He was a stunningly handsome boy with wavy, brown hair and dimples in his cheeks, and girls would take a great shine to him when they saw him in football togs, or in baseball uniform with "COLUMBIA" arching across his broad chest.

But the shine would rub off when they saw him hatless, coatless in his worn, patched clothes, and of course he didn't own a dinner jacket. Handsome as he was, the campus flames in most cases simply couldn't afford to be seen with a boy who didn't even have decent clothes. And besides, his mother was a sort of a cook, or chambermaid, or something in the fraternity house. Funny situation, eh? The girls preferred to skip it, and Gehrig skipped them. And the brothers, to a considerable extent skipped Lou. If Gehrig ever had a close man friend at Columbia, he never mentioned it to anyone.

What was happening was not exactly calculated to make the boy happy, or gregarious. On the contrary. He withdrew still further within himself. He became more shy and self-accusing. He was convinced that he was no good for anything and never would be.

5

A CAREER ENDED AND BEGUN

TIME lazily yawned past the golden statue of Alma Mater enthroned on Columbia's asphalt campus. A Major Bill Corum, youngest Major in the A. E. F. whose return from the battlefields of Europe was still fresh in the memory of the country, used to attend the School of Journalism and look out the window onto South Field, and watch a husky youngster with piano legs and dimpled cheeks endlessly shagging flies, or catching balls thrown at him by mates, and the Major, yet to become a top sports writer of the golden era to come, wondered about him, and who he was, and what made him chase and catch those balls eternally.

Lou Gehrig went out for baseball in the

spring and brought the lovelight to the eyes of Andy Coakley, Columbia coach and former pitcher for the Philadelphia Athletics. Andy made a pitcher out of him, took up the batting lessons where Kane had left off, and pretty soon Lou Gehrig was poling them high, wide and handsome over the college fences. He hit seven home runs in one season, one of them the longest ever seen at South Field, and batted over .540.

And he won himself a new name. They called him the "Babe Ruth of Columbia."

For the second time the shadow fell athwart him, though by now it was conceded to be an even greater honor, because the Babe had ushered in the year 1921 with 54 home runs, 1922 with 35, and 1923 with 41.

The Golden Decade was under way.

Then for the second time disaster in the form of illness struck at his home and his career, only this time it fell upon his mother, and Gehrig the boy was called upon to make a stern and important choice. He was young and simple, naive and boyish, and so he remained for most of his life, but over that one choice, the boy became a man.

A collegian who could sock a baseball as far as Gehrig was hitting them in the college games would naturally attract the attention of the Major League scouts, and Paul Kritchell, famous Yankee scout, saw enough of Gehrig to convince the management that he was worth signing.

Kritchell approached Andy Coakley and Gehrig, and Gehrig was excited and flattered, but all offers were turned down, because, to Momma Gehrig a man who did nothing but play games, even if it was for being paid money, was nothing but a loafer and a no good, and besides she was swelling with pride because her son was a "Collision" and a fraternity too, and she had helped him to do these things in spite of everything. Please God, as long as she had her health and strength, Lou should get an education as good as anybody in the country.

But it pleased God to try this family sorely, for it was her health and strength that failed when she contracted double pneumonia. Pop Gehrig was still sickly and unable to work. The little that Gehrig could bring in with his table waiting in the fraternity house and other odd jobs could not keep the family going, let alone pay the mounting doctor bills.

Life closed in on the Gehrigs. They were always close to the edge of things. Doctors and more doctors. Bills and more bills. Not a cent in the house, and nothing coming in.

There has been considerable discussion as to how much, in cold cash, Lou Gehrig actually cost the New York Yankees. According to Gehrig, he received $500 for making the momentous decision to sign a contract with organized baseball.

That $500 was the biggest sum of money that any of the Gehrigs had ever seen. It came at a time when it was desperately needed. It paid rent and doctors and hospital bills and nurses.

It represented a sacrifice made by Gehrig, freely and unheroically and untheatrically. For that sorely needed $500 he sold his right and his chance to go on into that other world around whose fringes he had played the last two years.

But one suspects from several things Gehrig said later, that that world no longer looked as attractive or worthwhile to him as it once had. Or that he was sorry to lose it. It is hard to get reserved and sensitive men to tell you what they really think and feel in their innermost beings. No one ever knew Lou Gehrig better or one tenth as well as his wife. And she says that the closest she could get to one of the toughest decisions a boy ever had to make and the manner of making it, is that it was simply thought of and simply done, too. Mom was ill and needed attention and there was no money and what would he care about an education if Mom died because he hadn't got her the right kind of care. That's all there was to it. Kritchell, the Yankee Scout, was there at the right time with the contract and the money, and Gehrig signed.

And having signed, he had to face a heartbroken and reproachful mother who could find it hard to forgive that her son for whom she had sacrificed so much to make him a *collision* should be going to become a bummer and a professional baseball player.

They probably yelled at one another after Mrs. Gehrig recovered and found out, because loud voices and yelling were part of the Gehrig household. But stripped of the commonplaces, the deed had nobility of which it cannot be robbed. It also was irrevocable.

There is an amusing story about the signing which may be apocryphal but the source is good.

The signing with the Yankees was kept se-

cret for a time and during this period, Wally
Pipp, the Yankee first baseman—who had
been playing on the team, as we remember,
when Gehrig was twelve, approached Lou on
the campus and made him an offer. A mid-
western National League Club had had its
eye on Gehrig's batting, and had empowered
Pipp to negotiate with him and offer him a
job as first baseman with the western club.

Gehrig blushed, and stammered, and kicked
the ground with his spikes, and said—"Aw,
gee, Mr. Pipp, that's awfully kind,—I'd like
to play for them, but I guess I'd better tell
you, I've signed to play with the Yankees."

Pipp went away and sought a bench to sit
down and cool off. The boy he had been trying to get for a national league club, might
eventually get his job at first base for the
Yankees away from him. Phew! Mr. Pipp
was practically psychic.

But there were to be many discouraging moments and frustrations before Gehrig was to

hear Miller Huggins say one spring—"All right, Gehrig. Get in there in place of Pipp."

Because for all of his big frame, loud voice and quick smile, Lou Gehrig was one of those strange souls born to be frustrated, to have glory and happiness always within his reach, yes, even to have it in his grasp, only to have it snatched away from him.

6

THOSE FABULOUS YANKEES

THE trick, in telling the story of the Yankees of 1926–7–8, is to keep away from the record book, inviting though it may appear with its orderly rows of figures and averages, ticketing the ability and performance of each man as though he were a horse. Record books always frightened me, though some people do not seem to be able to judge or visualize a ball player unless he has a mess of figures strung out after his name.

But my story of the Yanks of those glamor years shortly before the roof fell in upon the American financial structure, is that they were the hardest drinking, hardest hitting ball club in the history of the game, the most colorful and the most exciting to watch.

They had as their manager a sharp, dried up, mite of a man named Miller Huggins who was all wisdom and common sense and baseball brains. They had the dream pitching staff consisting of Pennock, Hoyt, Moore and Pipgras. There was Earl Combs, the lanky, fast Kentucky Colonel, Mark Koenig, the Swiss watch movement, Poosh-'em-op Tony Lazzeri and Jumping Joe Dugan.

And finally they offered that heart-breaking pair of ball busters, George Herman Ruth and Henry Louis Gehrig.

Did you ever see them play? Brother, you saw a ball team.

You also saw as grand and mad and wild, and goofy a collection of baseball ivory as was ever collected together under one tent.

This isn't designed particularly as a Sunday School take for tiny tots, so I'll tell you with considerable joy in the telling that the Yanks of those years were a drinking ball club. They like their likker. And they gave Miller Huggins many a headache. But drinks or no drinks, they won those pennants and those world series games, and they patted that apple.

Mark Koenig told me of a series in Chicago. The boys had been in a slump. Miller Huggins read them the riot act about their drinking and threatened to fire any man caught smelling of anything stronger than lilac water.

The boys loved Hug in their way, and his lectures always worked the first day. They swore off, and the next day played worse than ever. That night, Koenig said, you could see the boys sneaking out of their rooms at all hours and heading stealthily down the corridors and out of the hotel to return at dawn's early light, bearing with them some fine, first class packages.

But the next afternoon they were out of their slump and tearing into the hapless White Sox. The Yankee dugout smelled like a distillery, but Mister Huggins had eyes only for the relays of Sox pitchers who were being carted away one after the other, quietly gibbering. The little Miller also knew when to keep quiet.

Or there is the charming story of the pitcher who shall be Nameless, who was caught by Hug coming into the hotel at four A.M. one morning plastered, though still able to stand up. However, it should be recorded that this was only because a blonde was supporting him on one side and a red head on the other.

Huggins was an insomniac, made so by his worries as Yankee manager, and when he couldn't sleep he would get up and go walking. It was through this that the encounter took place.

Pitcher and Manager came face to face. Very quietly Huggins said, "Good morning, son."

The pitcher stared him right in the eye, smiled affably and said, "Hyyah, Hug!" They passed on.

The next morning, Huggins called in

brother Nameless, and let him have it. He bawled him out for the blonde, the carrot-top, both together, and for the condition he was in and said the next time that that happened it would cost him a fine and suspension.

Nameless didn't even argue. It was apparent that Hug had him dead to rights, color of female hair, quality of his breath and all. He just kept saying . . . "Okay, Hug. Okay. I'll try. I'll be all right."

When he got to the door at the end of the lecture, however, he turned around and said, "Hug, I'm gonna try to go straight. On the level. But there's just one thing I wanna know. Who is the so-and-so stool pigeon on this club?"

Those were the days. Drink, wench and clout the ball.

And what was Lou Gehrig doing on a team like that? How did he fit in? What was he like?

Why he was doing as he pleased. And it pleased him neither to drink, nor to wench, or to stay out late. And he nudged the pellet just the same, because life is like that. Some do and some don't. Lou liked his straight. And the other guys respected him for it. And they didn't kid him about it either. Because on a ball club, really to kid a guy you ought to be able to lick him in case he gets sore. And there wasn't anybody on the outfit who cherished notions of pushing Lou Gehrig around. But besides, nobody wanted to. If nothing else, it was a liberal crowd. Every guy could live according to his own notions as long as he continued to pole that pill for the communal good. When baseball is bread and butter, you never question a man's eccentricities as long as he continues to carry his weight and can hoist one into Railroad Street outside the park, when blue chips are down. I'm trying to give you a picture of those Yanks, and of Lou.

And I am also trying to give you an un-namby-pamby picture of baseball as it is, or at least as it was in those days. It isn't a game played for the sweet joy of sport by Sunday

School book characters, but a rough, competitive game played as a profession and a business by a bunch of tough, hard bitted men who were and are just like any other groups of men. In a group of twenty or thirty players you find all kinds. That Lou Gehrig was an ascetic, practically, in his manner of living, was purely a matter of his own personal choice. No one actually demanded it of him.

As a matter of fact, his wife relates, that once, and this was before they met, Lou was in a protracted slump and was miserable about it. Huggins who loved him like a son and who had an enormous influence upon his life, and all for the good, called him into his office, handed him a ten dollar bill and said . . . "For Pete's sakes, Lou, go out and get yourself a couple of drinks and some entertainment. You need loosening up."

Huggins was against ball players drinking heavily, but he was a superb psychologist, and he knew the relaxing effect of an occasional bender.

7

THE BITTER IMPATIENT DAYS OF TRIAL

ALTHOUGH Gehrig did not know it at the time he was farmed out to Hartford in the Eastern League for a couple of years, and in 1925, spent a lot of time sliding his pants up and down on the Yankee bench. Lou was and had been for some time a carefully planned sparkplug in the new baseball machine that Miller Huggins was building to replace the worn-out one that had won pennants in 1921–2–3. Ruth was still the big siege gun, but the rest of the team was getting old. Teams fall apart that way in spots, because most Major League teams are part seasoned veterans and part peppery youngsters. When the veterans go, replacements must be found and it is in those periods that the big teams will be found out of the money.

The team that took the field in 1925 at the beginning of the season was still the old Yankees whose infield consisted of Wallie Pipp, Pipp the Pickler, at first base, Aaron Ward at second, Deacon Everett Scott at short —the Scott who had hung up the consecutive games record of 1,307 games, which Gehrig broke August 17, 1933, and Jumping Joe Dugan at third.

But a glimpse of the Yankee line-up that took the field against the Cards in the World Series of 1926, shows only Joe Dugan still holding his job in the infield. The new kid infield was in. Lou Gehrig was on first, Tony Lazzeri . . . Poosh-'em-op Tony, on second and Mark Koenig at short.

This young infield had won the pennant for Huggins in one year, though it wasn't sufficiently seasoned to take the world series too. That came later in '27 and '28, when it won eight straight world series games from the Pirates and the Cardinals.

But when he chafed on the Yankee bench in

1925, Lou Gehrig, young and ambitious, had no picture of the long range view and the patient plans of such a master builder of championship ball teams as Miller Huggins. To Lou's young, ambitious impatient eyes, Wallie Pipp, toiling out there on first base was a fixture, as solid and immovable as Gibraltar.

Once, when Huggins was shipping some ivory off to St. Paul, Gehrig invaded Hug's room in the hotel, his bag all packed, and begged Hug to send him too. He was asking to be sent from a great Major League club, back to the minors, only so that he might be able to play ball. He was tired of sitting on the bench.

From Huggins that night, he got a lecture he never forgot. Hug said . . .

"Lou, I'm not going to send you off to St. Paul. You're going to stay right on that bench and learn baseball. You may think you know as much as those fellers out there on the field, but you don't. You got a lot to learn and there's no way to learn it right now except on the bench. Those fellers out there had to do the same thing when they were young. Your turn will come. I want you to sit next to me for a while on the bench. I'll help you."

It put an entirely new light on things for Lou. The bench no longer was a penance and a trial. It became a school. Sitting next to Huggins, he learned to appraise every batter that came to the plate, around the circuit, to memorize the placement of his hits, to note where Pipp played for him, how the infield lined up to handle him.

He learned to watch the pitchers, how they pitched, what they pitched, what their strategy was in a tight spot, their mannerism, little tell-tale give-away motions towards first, in short anything and everything that would help him to play the game when his time came. Baseball, he discovered, wasn't simply getting out there and stroking the ball out of the park and catching balls thrown at him. It was a painstaking profession, an exhausting and never ending study.

His chance came sooner than expected. In May, Pipp was beaned in batting practice and thereafter became subject to violent headaches. This fact gives rise to the story, probably apocryphal that one day when he complained of his head, Hug said . . . "Okay, Wallie . . . take a couple of aspirins and a seat on the bench," and sent Lou out to First Base.

At any rate, on June first, 1925, Lou Gehrig replaced Wallie Pipp. Thereafter for fourteen consecutive years and 2,130 consecutive games, he was never off First Base, except one game which he started as shortstop merely to be in the line-up and preserve his great consecutive games record at a time when he was bent double with lumbago.

But the story of what happened to Lou, that first game and what he said, does happen to be true. Running down to second base, he got into the line of the last half of a double play. The ball hit him squarely on the forehead and knocked him senseless.

They doused him with water and when he came to, he was asked whether he wanted to get out of the game. Lou looked up grimly and said . . .

"Hell no! It's taken me three years to get into this game. It's going to take more than a crack on the head to get me out."

How prophetic, tragically prophetic, his words were. His magnificent record of play survived beanings, fractures of toes and fingers, fevers, torn tendons, turned ankles, pulled muscles, lumbago, colds, and a host of minor mishaps that would have kept an average man in bed. He succumbed only to the crippling effects of an insidious and fatal disease, and even that he fought off in defiance of nature and the laws of medicine, for longer than it was thought possible.

But we are yet with young Lou on the

threshold of success, with Huggins sending him out onto the field with . . . "O. K., Lou, go on out there and play first. Hustle all the time, but don't get excited and do the best you can."

Hustle all the time!

That was the philosophy by which Lou Gehrig lived and died. I asked Ty Cobb for his definition of a "hustling" ball player. In his slow drawl, he said . . . "A hustlin' ball player is a feller who never lets up for a minute, never gives his body a rest from trying. He's out there every second of the time playing as hard as he can, no matter how many runs he's ahead. He don' know what it means to take it easy and loaf along. He's *ALWAYS* working. Lou Gehrig was the hustliest ball player I ever saw, and I admired him for it. When I first saw him break in the line-up, as a rookie, I went and told him just that."

So Lou had made the Yankees. Then he set

out to learn how to play first base. He was so anxious to learn, because he was such a clumsy Tanglefoot around that bag. He took advice from anyone and everyone, even Blind Tom, which is the ball players charm-name for the umpire.

Billy Evans, umpiring at First Base one time noticed a serious flaw in Lou's play shortly after he broke into the line-up. Bill took a chance of drawing a rebuke, because ball players were pretty touchy where umpires are concerned, but he said . . . "Young fellow . . . you're putting the wrong foot back on the bag."

Lou smiled at him and said . . . "Thanks, Mr. Evans. Watch me on the next play."

He got the proper foot back, but had to hesitate and think before he could do it. The next morning at ten o'clock he had Charley O'Leary the coach, out of bed and down to the field, practicing, until it became automatic.

Poor O'Leary. Gehrig practiced him rag-

ged. There was so much he had to learn about
fielding his position. Day in and day out, he
worked every morning from ten o'clock until
game time. He was weak on balls thrown into
the dirt. He made Charley throw balls at him
into the dirt until O'Leary's tongue was hang-
ing out. Lou did nothing naturally. Everything came the hard and tortuous way. Practice, practice, practice until he did it right,
and then practice some more to keep it right.

In the meantime, the Yankees were going
places. And so was Gehrig, and with him his
family.

These were great days for Mom, for Lou
took care of her.

He more than took care of her. He idol-
ized her. He brought her into the publicity
lime-light with him as his best girl and his
sweetheart. He bought her a fine house in
New Rochelle with his World Series earnings,
and made her mistress of it. Whenever anybody asked Lou about a girl or whether he had

a sweetheart he would say . . . "Yes, my Mom." And he would mean it. His early life had so molded him. Now, even in the growing days of his success, he was girl shy. His mother was all he wanted. He did not realize it, but this was to cause him heartache later when the thing happened he did not ever believe or dream would happen . . . that he would fall happily in love.

8

LOU AND BABE AND THE YANKS—
ONWARDS AND UPWARDS

BUT the time for the love story is not yet, though it must be told soon, because from now on the tale of Lou Gehrig is a continuous upward climb to fame and success beyond his dreams, the dreams of his mother, and certainly the wildest fancies of the sports writers who first saw him come up to the league as an awkward big, sterned, dimple cheeked Dutchman.

And did he rise! In 1925 a benchwarming rookie. In 1926 a hard hitting regular playing in a world series on a championship team. And in 1927 he was already daring to challenge Babe Ruth for the home run championship. Through half the season he ran neck and neck with the Great Man, homer for homer, until at the end Ruth pulled away. That was the year that George Herman set his record of 60 home runs. Gehrig scared or pushed him into it. The Babe got the credit all right, and in the final analysis it was he who had to lay the ash to those horserind balls, and the number two guy is just another fellow in the race. But it was Lou not only who made him do it out of sheer rivalry and competitive spirit, but who helped him to do it physically.

The boys who write the sports stories knew what was going on and who was doing what. On October 12, 1927, they voted Lou Gehrig the most valuable player in the American League.

You see, it was Lou Gehrig who forced the pitchers to pitch to Babe Ruth. Ever since Huggins had acquired the sensationally slugging Babe and the pitchers in self defense began to take some of the sensation out of him by walking him more than any batter has ever been walked before in the history of baseball, the little Miller had been looking for a Number 4 to bat behind Babe's No. 3. When Lou compiled his wonderful home run record with Hartford, Hug's head rested easy on his pillow o' nights, because he knew he was getting the answer to his prayers.

In 1926, the American League pitchers were unconvinced about Gehrig's hitting ability and still kept pitching those four wide ones to the Babe in times of crisis. Then Lou would come up and bust the lemon out of the county and there would go your old ball game.

By 1927 word went around the League . . . don't pass the Babe to get at Gehrig. Bad medicine. So they had to pitch to Babe. And the Babe got sixty home runs. But Lou got the valuable player award.

Would you like to know the true relationship between Ruth and Gehrig in those fine,

exciting, glittering days. They loved one another. Or rather Lou sincerely adored Ruth,
admired him, hero-worshipped him and
thought him a wonderful baseball player and
an amusing man. The Babe liked Lou insofar
as he was capable of loving anyone. It was
not until much, much later that they fell out.

Babe used to order Lou around and get
waited on by him, or send him to fetch. Lou
was such a self-effacing and modest man that
he saw nothing humiliating in such service,
which automatically *made* it non-humiliating.
The Babe was never much on remembering
names or telephone numbers . . . he couldn't
remember the names of the guys playing on his
own team, and so Lou used to be charged with
calling up the gals for Babe in the various
towns on the circuit, if the King felt in the
mood for a little gayety. The Babe's lusty
love of life, his appetites and his prowess with
wine, women and food was always a source of
enormous amusement to Lou. He just didn't

care about taking part, because that is the kind of a man he happened to be. They got on excellently well together, once even rooming together (an idea of Hug's who hoped that Lou would hold Babe down a little). But two more opposite types were never on any one ball club.

With regard to their rivalry, and the way Babe felt about it, an article appeared in Liberty in 1933, signed by Lou Gehrig in which Lou quotes Babe Ruth as saying to him during a confidential mood in 1927 at the time of their home run race ... "Say, young fellow, there's a lot of fun in this thing but the money is the thing we're after. It's all over there ..." and here he pointed to the boundaries of the Yankee Stadium ... "Back of those fences! That's where the money is. The more balls we hit over the wall, the more world series we'll get. Suppose we forget each other and remember that."

It sounds like the kind of thing the Babe

might have said. But also remember that the Babe did hit sixty that year. There is no doubt in my mind that great competitor that Ruth was, he felt the sting of Gehrig's youthful drive keenly. And in later years when Gehrig surpassed him in everything but home run hitting and had become the darling of the press, while Ruth was slipping, I am sure that he grew a little jealous of him. What would that be but human? And what was Babe if not intensely human at all times?

They were a brutal crew of ball wreckers, those Yanks, and they did fabulous things.

Picture yourself a pitcher trying to get by Murderer's Row. First up was Combs, a sharp eyed hitter, long legged and fast as a whippet. One mistake and you'd have Combs sitting on first. Koenig was up next, a precision machine at getting a man along to second with hit or sacrifice. And by that time you were shaking anyway, because Babe Ruth was approaching. And if you got by Ruth you had to whip Gehrig who was even more dangerous because whereas Babe was just as apt to strike out as hit a home run, Lou was a wonderful all-around hitter. And then you still couldn't relax a tired arm or quivering nerve, because you got Bob Meusel after Gehrig, and Tony Lazzeri who was also no slouch with his funny sliding swing that could park a ball in the bleachers. Then came Bengough, or Collins, the catchers. All the Yankee pitchers could hit, especially Waite Hoyt. And then it started all over again.

Nineteen twenty seven was the year that the Yanks went to Pittsburgh to play the Pirates in a world series. The Pirates had the Waner Boys and were cocky. To deflate them a little, Huggins sent Ruth and Gehrig into the batting cage to indulge in a little pre-game hitting practice. Babe and Lou at Miller's suggestion put on one of the greatest hitting shows ever seen when they knocked pitch after pitch over the fence, over the bleachers and over the roof. Of course a batting practice pitcher was serving them up and putting them right down the middle, but it was the terrible demonstration of power that broke the spirit of the Pirates before they ever took the field. They lost the series in straight games.

The next year, the Yanks met St. Louis again and beat them four straight with Lou and Babe blasting the Redbirds into nervous wrecks with a bombardment of home runs. Lou got four home runs, the Babe three. The Babe got all three of his in one game, the last. Two of his, Lou got in one game. He was shooting for Babe's mark of three in one game, to please his mother who was in the stands, but the St. Louis pitcher walked him the last two times.

9

"STRIKE OUT YOU BIG GOOF"—IT WAS LOVE!

LIFE went on. Lou gained in stature and ability. His mother kept house for him, and continued to play the role of his sweetheart. And he seemed to be a boy who was happy and content with life.

He *WAS* happy too, but those who knew him in those years and understood him knew also that he was a lonely boy. His pleasures were few. He loved to go fishing, and he used to come home and take his mother fishing with him off New Rochelle, or drive out to Long Island and fish for flounders.

But somehow, the truest picture of the loneliness that was in his soul I get from the friend of his who told me that in those days he used to go up to Rye Beach where there was an amusement park and ride on the roller coaster all by himself for hours.

He just didn't go for girls, though he occasionally took one out to the movies. Shortly before he died, Miller Huggins asked Lou why he didn't find some nice girl, marry her and have a home. Lou's answer was typical. He didn't think he would ever find a girl who would have him. He was content with his mother. No girl would possibly want to have a guy like him.

Hug's death in 1929 came as a great shock to Lou and he found himself lonelier than ever. Joe McCarthy who succeeded Huggins as Yankee Manager was always fond of Lou and became a great friend, but there was something paternal about his relation with Huggins.

Time passed. Murderer's Row gave way to the Bronx Bombers. The Yankee line-up now read . . . Combs, Sewell, Ruth, Gehrig, Laz-

zeri, Dickey, Chapman and Crosetti. Mc-
Carthy was setting up his first championship
team and it was built around the slugging of
Lou Gehrig now, more than the power of
Ruth, which was beginning to wane a little.

In 1932, the Yankees won the Championship again. That was the year when on July
3rd, in Philadelphia, Lou Gehrig hit four
home runs in one game. And in the fall, Lou
Gehrig was the undisputed hero of the world
series in which the Yanks beat the Cubs four
straight, and Babe Ruth made his last and
most dramatic bid for immortality by pointing
out to the Cubs pitcher the exact spot in cen-
terfield where he was going to paste the next
service for a home run. And then doing it.

It was so typical of the Ruth-Gehrig over-
shadowing that by a single gesture, Ruth made
everybody forget that Gehrig hit two home
runs that day, both off the first pitch delivered
by Root, Cub star. Lou's second home run
followed right on the heels of Babe's dramatic move. Nobody even saw that one.

Even if he was still somewhat under Babe's shadow, Gehrig had the recognition of the ball players and the sports writers. He was getting more money each year. And the more money he got, and the more fame, the more lonely he grew too. There was no one with whom to share it, no one who could really rejoice with him. The big man, now in his twenty-ninth year was starved for affection.

But he was just one year away from meeting the girl who was destined to give him the happiest and richest years of his life.

Eleanor, however, had seen Lou several times before they met. And she tells it charmingly:

"I first saw Lou Gehrig in the summer of 1932," Eleanor Gehrig told me. "I hated him. I hated all the Yankees. I was a White Sox rooter. I sat there in the ball park and hoped Gehrig would fall down and break a leg. Once I yelled at him, 'Strike out, you big goof!'"

In this manner began the love story of Lou

and Eleanor Gehrig, though they did not meet until sometime later.

Eleanor Twitchell was born in Chicago in 1905, of a family of considerable means. Her father was the caterer for the Park system in Chicago and had the concession for refreshments in five large parks. She was brought up in an atmosphere of comparative wealth . . . her family owned three cars, horses, city and country homes.

She was pretty in a fresh, round-faced sort of way with rich brown hair and sweet eyes. At 23 she was a gay, light hearted creature with considerable impish humor, many friends and nothing to do but go horseback-riding, play golf and go to parties. She was fond of music, had studied the piano and after leaving school, continued an interest in applied psychology, which interest she carefully concealed from the gay, irresponsible crowd of pre-1928 playboys with which she surrounded herself.

The crash of 1929 wrecked the family fortunes and blew her gay, dizzy, play-world out from under her.

Before the smoke of explosion had cleared and the debris came drifting back to earth, Eleanor Twitchell had popped herself into a secretarial school. It was her own idea. Everything she did from then on was her own idea. And they were ideas that had as a basis an instinct for sound and simple common sense and understanding of values. She moved quietly over from play-girl to working girl overnight.

When Lou Gehrig was first introduced to her at a party in Chicago, in 1933, Eleanor had a secretarial job with the lighting engineer of the World's Fair in Chicago. Babe Ruth was there as well as a few other ball players. Eleanor remembers that she was rather impressed with the all-over gargantuan qualities of George Herman Ruth. Of Gehrig she neither saw nor remembered much.

That, you see, was one of the characteristics of the pattern of Lou Gehrig's life. Nobody much saw or remembered his deeds or personality as long as Babe Ruth was around.

Later in 1933, at another gathering they met again. And this time something happened to the quiet, self-conscious athlete. He noticed Eleanor Twitchell. Something about her called to something within him and he tried to be with her during the evening. But each time he managed to get to her side, something intervened. Another swain moved Eleanor away, a bridge game was started, or there would be dancing.

They talked a little. The antennae of Eleanor's instincts began to yield messages broadcast by the silent boy. He was so unlike the other ball players. His voice was loud and gross, but his soul was meek and sensitive and sweet. The muscles of his back bulged out the lines of his coat. Shy melancholy and unexpressed yearning illuminated his eyes.

When later in the evening Eleanor tried to find him to match up the rather haunting impression he had made upon her, he had gone home to his hotel. As always he was in strict training and went to bed early to be well slept out for the game the next day.

The party broke up quite late. Eleanor couldn't forget the big guy with the dimples, the wavy hair and the smitten eyes. The other girls were saying, "Gee, Eleanor! What did you do to Gehrig? He never looks twice at a girl and you had him following you around all evening."

But Eleanor didn't need the girls to tell her that Gehrig had been interested. What intrigued and then bothered her was that SHE was feeling a little strange herself.

And on an impulse, at four o'clock in the morning she called Gehrig up at his hotel. She thought perhaps if she said . . . "I just wanted to say . . . 'Good night' to you, because I missed saying it at the party," he might

take a hint and say something like . . .
"Couldn't we get together some time soon so
that we *can* say good night," etc.

To put it as Eleanor succinctly phrased it
. . . "It certainly worked out swell."

She heard a fuzzy, sleep-sodden voice say
. . . "Hello!" She then made her speech.
There was a mild crash as Lou apparently
knocked things off the night table while at-
tempting to put on the light, and then a horri-
fied gasp . . . "Good God! Do you know
what time it is?"

This was followed by the unmistakable
click of the receiver being replaced in its
cradle.

And that, thought Eleanor, is that.

The next morning at her office in the Fair
Grounds she had the shock of her life. She
was telephoning and happened to look out of
the window. It was shortly after nine o'clock.
Lou was standing down on the sidewalk grin-
ning up at her and waving enticingly to her to
come down.

Eleanor was on second base, so to speak, but she had got there, by what in baseball parlance is known as a delayed steal. It had taken no more than four or five hours for it to penetrate through Lou's Germanic skull that maybe this girl liked him a little if she took the trouble to call him up so early in the morning.

Eleanor reports that she snapped her French heels and burst a shoulder strap getting down there before he could get away. They had lunch. They had dinner. They spent the evening wandering about the Fair. Lou was a very shy man. They went on the roller coaster together. When they came to the big drop where the least a girl could expect was an arm around, he clutched the handrail of the rocket car with both hands and hollered . . . "Hang on, Eleanor, this is a beaut."

When she tried delicately to steer him to the dark and cozy confines of the Red Mill he sidetracked her to the baseball bathing booth and the concession where you knock things off shelves with baseballs. He cleaned out both booths, nearly wrecking them, completely exhausted himself, covering himself with sweat, grime and glory, and his Eleanor he buried beneath a mountain of hideously painted bisque Kewpie dolls and rag horses.

It was Lou's small boy's way of showing that he cared.

They began writing to one another. Eleanor visited him in his home at New Rochelle and met the family, during the winter. When Lou returned to Chicago with the Yankees on their first Western swing in 1933, he proposed to his Eleanor and she accepted him.

It wasn't quite as simple as that, though, because Lou was so shy and inhibited and so super conscious of his own lack of worth. He was desperately in love with Eleanor and she knew it. What woman doesn't? She also knew that she was vitally in love with him. And she was unquestionably the stronger of the two.

The February before they became engaged,

Lou had a hold-out session with the Yankees and he wrote to Eleanor that he was determined to fight out his differences with Ruppert even if he never played baseball again, claiming that he could always drive a truck or become a good chauffeur.

With extraordinary wisdom, Eleanor began to build up his self confidence. Her love had diagnosed his case at once. She began to impress him with some sense of his values and importance, made him see that not only was he a man of great personal charm, but that he was also a great figure in the world of sports, Ruth or no Ruth.

Gehrig proposed to Eleanor at her home in Chicago, and Eleanor said that it was difficult to get it out of him. He fumbled and garbled words, and went through all the sweet agonies of a shy man trying to declare himself. Eleanor helped him. She said she was practically finishing his sentences for him. She also said that he probably got the quickest "YES" on record.

10

THE COURSE AND THE OBSTACLE

THE obstacle to the course of this simple love story was Mom. Mom had been queen too long. The newspapers the length and breadth of the land had written of her and pictured her as Lou's sweetheart. It was only human that she resented "that girl from Chicago."

We have seen how as Lou rose to success he took his mother along with him down the rosy paths of publicity and fame. In short, he spoiled her. She was unable to give way gracefully to the girl from Chicago who in addition to being an interloper and Lou's dearly beloved was also modern in her ways and her views.

Although Lou was thirty and was making a

considerable amount of money, his love affair had to be conducted almost clandestinely. If they wanted to be alone together they would have to sneak off to achieve it. Mom did not mean to be a nuisance. It was just that she could not bear to be left out in the cold where Lou was concerned.

And much as Lou loved his mother, his adoration of his Elcanor was out of this world. All the affection that had been denied him as a child, all the limitless affection he had to give on his own part and which had never had a chance to expand, came to a head in and about Eleanor.

Strong as Mom was, Lou was stronger when it came to his determination to marry Eleanor, and the wedding was set for September, 1933, at the Long Island home of a friend of Eleanor's.

They were to live in an apartment in New Rochelle so as to be near Mom. Mom of course couldn't understand why Lou didn't go on living in the house with them so that she could cook and look after him as usual.

There must have been some sort of argument, or quarrel, or family row over Eleanor, because one morning, Lou came over to the apartment where Eleanor in a house dress, smudged and work-dirty, with her hair down over her eyes and her nose shiny, was supervising the work of carpenters, plumbers, painters, electricians and carpet layers.

Lou was in a sweat and a panic that somehow he might lose Eleanor if he did not marry her at once, that Mom, or something or somebody would do something to interfere. Or perhaps he was just suffering from that fear to which much-in-love grooms-to-be are prone, that any moment, the desired one is liable to vanish into thin air and never never return.

At any rate, big, loud, tumultuous Lou came huffing and stamping into the house and said:

"El . . . why can't we be married right

away now? You know I can't go for one of
those stiff Long Island weddings. How would
I look at one of those? It's just between us, anyway, El, and why do we have to wait? I don't
know what Mom is liable to do when she gets
excited. Let's do it now."

Eleanor had rather wanted that Long Island
wedding. She had been looking forward to it.
But she understood her man, and what is more
she loved him. She understood that this pro-
posal of a quick, do-it-now marriage was more
than just the impatience of a lusty swain. Lou
was declaring himself out from the parental
nest and was doing a job of untying the apron
strings to which he had bound himself for so
long. She knew that he felt that once he had
her legally that he would feel safe. And
whatever qualms she had about what life
would be like, wedded to all the Gehrigs, they
vanished now. Here was a boy who with her
help and guidance would stand squarely on his
own feet.

They went into a whirlwind of action and within two hours, her friend was over from Long Island, Fred Lindner, a pal of Lou's who lived in White Plains drove over, and the Mayor of New Rochelle climbed into his cutaway official stovepipe. Lou was in an open shirt, Eleanor in her housedress. The ceremony began. The plumber and his helper shouted . . . "Watch it there! Comin' through!" and marched through the wedding bearing a radiator to be installed, the carpenters hammered, the electricians threaded their wires and tested bells and buzzers, the Mayor intoned with dignity . . . "Do you, Lou, take this girl Eleanor, in sickness and in health, in . . ."

At which point, a pop-eyed carpet layer suddenly looked up, spit out a mouthful of tacks and yelled . . . "Hey, fellers! Ya know what's going on here? Lou Gehrig's bein' married right under our nose."

Work stopped. All the men crowded

around, took off their hats respectfully and stood in attendance while Lou and Eleanor were joined together in holy matrimony.

And then they just made the Yankee Stadium in time, thanks to motorcycle escort provided by the Mayor. For marriage or not, it wouldn't do for Lou to miss the starting lineup. He was in the way of having quite a record for consecutive games played.

It is recorded that out of sheer exuberance, and the sight of his wife sitting in a field box with a wedding band on her finger, Lou rode one out of the park that day.

11

HAPPILY EVER AFTER

AND so they were married and lived happily ever after.

Or at least, they lived happily, because the shadow of their tragedy was not yet over them. Lou who had never known much gayety or frivolity began to learn to enjoy life.

If you want to know how a ball player lives when he is at home, I can give you Lou Gehrig's time table.

Up at ten in the morning for a large breakfast, or brunch, since he would not eat again until evening, consisting of three or four eggs with bacon or ham, sausages on the side, with wheatcakes, toast, fruit and coffee. He left for the ball park at noon so as to be there for batting practice which started at 1 P.M. Usually Eleanor went with him. The game would be over around five in the afternoon when they would drive home. They rarely went out to dinner during the season. Lou liked to eat at home, and more, he liked to be in Eleanor's company. He liked people, but he seemed to be jealous once he was married, jealous of every moment that deprived him of the company of his girl. He had been so long finding her. It had, so he thought, been such a precarious exploit, winning her. (Eleanor said: "Actually he would have had to have shot me to have got rid of me, or escaped me.") And so he was quite content to be alone with her. After dinner they would go to a movie, though in later years, Lou developed a deep and honest love and appreciation of fine music and used to like to go to concerts.

But for the flavor of the marriage, you must come with me into their home, and see this big guy with the loud voice, the bright friendly eyes and the dimples at the corners of his mouth, stamping into the house like a half-tamed earthquake and yelling for his dinner.

"Hey Pal! What's for eating? Got any Hamburgers? Yeeeeow! I gotta have Hamburgers!" Then he would storm into the kitchen and lift up all the tops of the pots and see what was cooking.

Lou wasn't foul mouthed or a curser, though he could refer to someone as a sonova-bitch, in the normal, even course of conversation, but he always smiled when he said it.

At home he was as playful as a big dog. He'd call for his Eleanor with a howl of . . . "Where's the old bat? Hey, Hag, come on out here and fight like a man."

To him she was the old bat, the old bitch, the bag and the battle-axe, but when people were around he called her "Pal," or "My pal!"

He was always "Lou" to her, except in the more earnest moments of baiting one another when he became The Monster, Dracula, or Frankenstein.

Gehrig was full of spirits and loved rough house, and big as he was, he and Eleanor would wrestle on the floor, pull each other's hair, or even box. Once, by accident, Eleanor let one go and caught Lou right on the button. He went down and stayed down. When he got unfuzzed a few seconds later, his laughter nearly took the roof off the house.

They were close mentally and physically. Gehrig never talked about his baseball exploits at home. He would talk about what "We" or the team had done, but never of his own individual achievements.

Eleanor was always thinking up ways of amusing him, and Lou adored it, and her for it. When he travelled, he would always get off the train at Harmon, and she would drive over from Larchmont where they moved to, and pick him up. It was a never failing ritual. Once when he arrived, the car was there with a chauffeur, but no Eleanor. Lou was furious. He burned to a crisp. Then he grew morose. It was obvious that Eleanor didn't love him anymore otherwise she wouldn't have forgotten him to play bridge or gab with females.

He got into the car. Two miles down the road, two outlandish-looking females with long red noses, and Victorian costumes stood by the side of the road, thumbing Lou's car for a ride. When the chauffeur stopped they piled in and all over Lou. It was Eleanor and a girl friend.

Slowly, and with infinite patience, as the marriage grew in strength and beauty, Eleanor brought him along, little by little, to improve his dressing and his tastes. Whereas, when they first met he went only to bad movies, after three years or four years he had progressed to where he loved good shows, concerts, opera and dining out at places like "21."

He had no interest in money other than something to be used to gain security for his family and Eleanor. He never questioned his wife's bills. For himself, the only things he ever spent money on was fishing tackle. He loved any kind of fishing, deep sea preferred, chasing the big stuff with rod and reel, but when that wasn't practical, or possible, he was just as content to bottom fish for flounders with handlines, or gig for eels.

Once he wanted a second hand fishing boat. It was only $175. But before closing the deal he went home first and talked it over with Eleanor, wondering whether it would be all right for him to buy it. It was little things like that that used to break Eleanor's heart. She was a creature who got much joy out of life and she wanted her husband to have his joys too. But it was hard to get him to take them. His old habits of self denial were hard to break or even soften.

And further to feel their marriage . . .

they quarrelled, or rather had spats like all people, and were hurt for a little while, and then made up. But there was a curious quality to their differences. Eleanor might speak impatiently or sharply to Lou about something. And Lou wouldn't speak to her for three days. And Eleanor would go around frightened to death, saying to herself . . . "Now I've gone and done it. Why did I have to say that? He's probably so mad at me he's getting ready to walk out. Twitchell, why can't you keep your big mouth shut?"

But Gehrig, it would turn out, wasn't angry. HIS silence would be the result of a morose conviction that Eleanor was about to leave HIM. He would say . . . "Gee, El, I don't understand, honestly, why you keep on with a mug like me. Why don't you get yourself some regular fellow and not waste your time with a sap who does nothing but make you unhappy all the time? I'm just no good, and I know it. I don't deserve you. I'm just a miserable Sourpuss who continually causes you grief and hasn't the qualifications to hold your respect. . . ."

Two minutes of that and Eleanor would be in tears and would have to start building him up all over again and tell him how wonderful he really was to her. And the perpetual honeymoon would get a fresh start. Life was never really dull around the Gehrigs. And the bitter tragedy they were eventually called upon to face and which they did face so gallantly was still far away.

12

THE FULL MEASURE OF SUCCESS

SUCCESS now came to Henry Louis Gehrig, the American born son of immigrant German parents, success in full measure.

His struggles, as it were, had ended. He had fame, money, popularity, love and companionship, and, thanks to his wife, even a little self assurance.

The boy who had been something of a rough, uncultured ball player with tastes that seldom rose above a "B" movie, found his interest awakened in music, books and the theatre. To what is at best an abnormal life —that of the itinerant baseball player—his wife brought as much normalcy as possible.

The awkward boy who could neither bat nor field as a youngster, had by his unswerving persistency, his gnawing ambition, tenacity and iron will power, made himself into the greatest first baseman in the history of organized baseball.

I remember writing years ago about Gehrig . . . "To my mind there is no greater inspiration to any American boy than Lou Gehrig and his career. For if the awkward, inept and downright clumsy Gehrig, that I knew and saw in the beginning, could turn himself into the finest first base covering machine in all baseball, through sheer drive and determination, then nothing is impossible to any man or boy in this country."

Men like Connie Mack and Hughie Fullerton, hoary baseball encyclopedias, who spanned generations of players, unhesitatingly placed Lou Gehrig at first base on any "All" team.

When the "All Star" games were played each summer, there was bitter controversy about many of the positions and who should play them. But it was almost automatically conceded that Lou Gehrig should play first base for the American Leaguers.

In 1934 Lou won the triple batting championship of the American League, and gave it to his Eleanor for the First Anniversary present. He led the League in hitting that year, batting .363, hitting 49 home runs, and driving in 165 runs.

It is interesting to note Ruth's waning record for the same year. He hit .288, knocked 22 out of the park, and batted in 84 runs.

In 1935, Lou Gehrig was out from beneath the shadow of Babe Ruth. The Babe was no longer with the Yankee team. The playing days of the Great Man were over. Wear and Tear and Time had tapped Ruth. But actually, Gehrig had begun to emerge even before Ruth's retirement into the golden pages of baseball history. For towards the end, as the figures indicate, not even the Babe could cast a shadow large enough to blanket the Iron Horse.

Gehrig's modesty and self depreciation continued to keep him in the background, but his deeds, his amazing vitality, durability and the quality of his play refused to be submerged any longer.

Sincere tributes and appreciations of the man began to appear in the columns and the sports pages. The sports writers began to look down from the Olympian slopes of the press box at the piano legs, the broad and honest rear porch which had earned him the name of Biscuit Pants, the powerful, smooth-swinging shoulders, and the young and pleasant face of "that big dumb Dutchman," with honest and deep affection.

Success! The Golden Decade was buried in the limbo of beautiful dreams. There was a new era and a new team. The Bronx Bombers had supplanted Murderer's Row, and was carving out its own record. They won the American League pennant in 1936–7–8. They won three World Series championships in a row, two from the Giants, beating them four games to two and four games to one. And the third they took from the helpless Cubs, four straight.

Yes, it was a wonderful, gleaming, glittering golden success. Lou was in the thick of it, driving in the runs, clouting the potato out of the ballyard, fielding for position, winning new honors, breaking and setting new records.

In 1936, Lou was again named the most valuable player in the American League, exactly nine years after he had first achieved this honor. His salary had been mounting steadily too, and in 1938 he signed for the largest sum he ever received for playing ball—$39,000.

And in the meantime, his consecutive games record was going on and on as though it would never stop. He celebrated his 1,500th game, his 1,800th, his 1,900th and his 2,000th.

And in connection with the last there hangs a little inside story. Christy Walsh who managed Gehrig's extra-curricular earnings, told it to me. Christy, you may remember, was the Spook of Spooks, the Father of the Ha'nt or Ghost system of sports writing, operating a sports syndicate from which issued a steady stream of platitudes bearing the 18 karat Hancocks of Babe Ruth, Lou Gehrig, the late Knute Rockne, and dozens of others.

As the 2,000th game approached, Walsh tried to persuade Gehrig to stay away from it and go fishing. He maintained—and it was a brilliant publicity stroke—that if Lou stopped at 1,999 games, it was a figure no one could forget. Whereas no one would remember how many games past 2,000 he played. And the story would make Page One. The idea of course was to impart some Ruthian vermilion to the somewhat pastel shades of Gehrig.

They sold it to Gehrig too. Until the day came. And then he couldn't go through with it. He couldn't let the club down. He couldn't disappoint the people who would come to see him play his two thousandth game. And besides a pennant race was on. He had to play in every game.

When Christy Walsh mentioned color again, Lou exploded . . . "If I have to do nutty things to have color, I don't want to have any. Why can't I just be myself?"

It was Eleanor who said quietly . . . "Lou, you're smarter than all the rest of us put together. You just go on being yourself, and never be anything else. Because that's the guy that people love."

"To Thine Own Self Be True," is a potent motto that hangs on many a classroom wall, but Gehrig demonstrated it, simply and naturally, where a lot of people could see and appreciate it; grown-ups as well as kids. He refused to be anything but himself, a simple, earnest, honest, conscientious soul.

13

"WHAT'S THE MATTER WITH GEHRIG?"

TOWARDS the end of the last decade, the name, the figure, and above all, the simple engaging personality of Lou Gehrig became welded into the National scene. Came the baseball season, came Gehrig. Came Gehrig, came home runs, triples, doubles, excitement and faultless play around First Base. And his record ran on. Day in day out he played, sick or well, never missing a game.

Sick or well. I wonder whether you know what that means to a ball player, and particularly one who plays at First Base where the bumps are many and there is daily physical danger both from ball and man.

He played with colds. He played with fevers. He played so doubled over with the torture of lumbago that it was impossible for him to straighten up, and bent over at the plate, he still played and he still got himself a single.

In 1934, the year he won the triple crown, he fractured a toe. He played on. He was knocked unconscious by a wild pitch, suffered a concussion that would hospitalize the average man for two weeks. He was at his position the next day and collected four hits.

When his hands were X-rayed, late in his career, they found seventeen assorted fractures that had healed by themselves. He had broken every finger of both hands and some twice, and *hadn't even mentioned it* to anyone. The fantastic thing about this is that not only was he able to endure the pain of breaks, strains, sprains, pulled and torn tendons, muscles and ligaments, but they failed to impair his efficiency. On the contrary, if he had something the matter with him it was the signal for him to try all the harder so that no one, and least of all his own severe conscience, could accuse him of being a handicap to his team while playing in a crippled condition.

When in 1939, Lou Gehrig found himself unaccountably slow in spring training, he began to punish his body for a failure that was unaccountable and to drive it harder and more mercilessly than ever before.

It had begun before that, the slow tragedy of distintegration. Signs and symptoms had been mistaken. During most of 1938, Gehrig had been on a strict diet. Thirty-eight had not been a good year for him. In the early winter of 1939 he had taken a $5,000 salary slash. Baseball players are paid by the records they compile.

And in the winter of 1939 Lou and Eleanor as usual, went ice skating together. Lou was a fine skater. But, strangely, he kept falling all the time.

The teams went south for the 1939 training season and the sports writers went along with them. And the boys with one voice began sending back stories that must have saddened them to write. I know sports writers. When you grow to love an athlete the way they did love Lou Gehrig, it isn't fun to oil your typewriter with his blood and be the first to write the story of the passing from the sports scene of a once great figure.

It is rather shocking to see all the stories gathered together on two or three of the large pages of Lou Gehrig's scrapbook compiled by his wife. They ask . . . "What is the matter with Gehrig?"

And having asked, they answered it. They wrote that Gehrig was through. They hated to do so, but they owed a loyalty to their papers and to the people who read the papers. An honest reporter writes what he sees.

What they saw was not unfamiliar to them. The useful playing lifetime of a top flight professional athlete is on the average shockingly short. A sports writer lives through many generations of them. He becomes alert to notice the first symptoms of slowing up. They were obvious with Gehrig at St. Petersburg. He was slow afoot, afield and at bat. And while he fought like a rookie to hold his position there was no improvement evident. Sadly they wrote that Lou was going the way of all athletes. His race was run. He might speed up when they hit the warmer weather of the regular season, but the old Iron Horse was running down.

But the players on the Yankee ball club were saying something else. The sports writers were looking through the wire mesh of the batting screens. Gehrig's colleagues were close to him—close enough to touch. They noticed things, strange things that were happening to their captain, things that worried and depressed them. And they had knowledge too, of their craft and of themselves. One of the things they knew was that a ball player slows up only gradually. His legs go, imperceptibly at first, then noticeably as he no longer covers the ground in the field that he used to cover. But he doesn't come apart all at one time, and in chunks.

I talked to Tony Lazzeri at his sweet, neat little home in San Francisco, where he now plays with the Seals. Tony watched Lou in practice in Florida in 1939. Once Lou was up at the plate and ducked back from a close one. And he couldn't stop himself. He just kept on staggering backwards, unable to regain his balance, until he crased into one of the other players who righted him again.

Ball players knew that wasn't right.

Bill Dickey, Lou's closest friend, was worried sick. He began to watch over Lou the way a father watches over a child. . . . And nobody would say anything to Gehrig, because rough and tough the ball player may be, but he is a sensitive fellow and a great respecter of private feelings.

There are grim tales of things that happened in the locker room, and one is dreadfully macabre with overtones of fine manly nobility. It is of Gehrig dressing, leaning over to lace his spikes and falling forward to the floor to lie there momentarily helpless. And it tells further of tough men with the fine instincts to look away and not to hurt his already tortured soul the more by going to him or offering to help. Quickly they left the locker room leaving him to struggle to his feet alone with no eyes to see his weakness.

They knew that it wasn't age that was bothering Gehrig, but that he was sick.

14

PORTRAIT OF COURAGE

FEW men can have gone through the hell that Gehrig did during those hideous days.

If you ask me what are some of the elements that go to make up what the populace terms or selects as a hero, I would say, among other things, the capacity for quiet, uncomplaining suffering, the ability to take it and never to let on, never to let the world suspect that you are taking it.

This was Lou Gehrig. Not even his wife knew wholly, though she must have suspected, how terribly Gehrig suffered during those days when his speed and skill were deserting him and his once iron muscles suddenly housed a tragic mystery that turned them to useless rags.

Can you not picture the fear, the worry, the helpless bewilderment that must have filled Lou's soul as he found that he could not bat, he could not run and he could not field? Life for him took on all the aspects of the most horrid of nightmares. All the fear-dreams to which humans are prone, dreams of shameful failure, dreams of not being able to run when pursued, dreams of performing some well-remembered daily office with most grotesque results, now haunted his waking hours.

The strain and terror of it lined his face in a few short months and brought grey to his hair. But it could not force a complaint to his lips.

Gehrig's most powerful reaction when it became apparent that there was something wrong with him, was to drive himself still further, still harder, to punish his flagging muscles and sick body relentlessly.

He was certain that it was work he needed that fatal spring training session of 1939. He drove himself furiously, castigated and punished himself. He took it out on the body that

had for so long been his willing and sometimes, it must be confessed, abused slave. It
never occurred to him that something entirely
different might be the matter with him or to
blame for his apparent lack of physical condition, something quite outside his own powers
to control.

His performance during the early part of
1939 was pitiful compared to the man who
had been. And yet, strangely, so great was the
spell that his integrity, his honest attempts to
please and his service over the long years, had
cast over the baseball world, that that worst
mannered, most ill-tempered and boorish man
in the world, the baseball fan, forbore to
heckle him.

On Sunday, April 30, 1939, the Yankees
played the Senators in Washington. Lou
Gehrig came to bat four times with runners
on base. He failed to get a hit, or even meet
the ball, and the Yankees lost.

Something else happened on that day.

There was a toss ball at first. The pitcher fielded a one-hop grounder, ran over towards first and tossed the ball underhand to Lou, as pitchers frequently do when there is time.

Lou muffed the throw.

Monday was an off day. Lou went to Larchmont. He did a lot of thinking. But he did the thinking to himself. He had the toughest decision of his life to make. But he had to make it alone.

Tuesday, May 2nd, the team met in Detroit to open a series against the Tigers. Joe McCarthy flew in from Buffalo. Lou met him in the dugout and said the fateful words:

"Joe, I always said that when I felt I couldn't help the team any more I would take myself out of the line-up. I guess that time has come."

McCarthy said: "When do you want to quit, Lou?"

Gehrig looked at him steadily and said, "Now. Put Babe Dahlgren in."

[143]

Later, alone in a corner of the dugout he wept.

The streak ended at 2,130 games.

The newspapers and the sports world buzzed with the sensation of his departure from the line-up of the Yankees.

Lou, at the urging of Eleanor, went up to the Mayo Clinic at Rochester, Minnesota, for a check-up.

There was a lull in the news. The sensation of Gehrig's withdrawal from the game he had played for so long died down.

Then out of a clear sky the storm burst again. Black headlines tore across the page tops like clouds, and lightninged their messages. . . . "GEHRIG HAS INFANTILE PARALYSIS." . . . "GEHRIG FIGHTS PARALYZING ILLNESS."

The New York Yankees released the report of the Doctors at the Clinic. It was a disease diagnosed as Amyothropic Lateral Sclerosis, interpreted for the layman as a form of Infantile Paralysis, and the mystery of the too sudden decline and passing of Louis Henry Gehrig, perennial Yankee First baseman, was solved.

The people who loved and respected Gehrig, or who merely knew of him as a great athlete and an outstanding performer, read with sympathy the newspaper stories to the effect that with care and treatment he would have a 50–50 chance to triumph over the disease, and that even running its course it would not affect him too badly, and though his playing days were over, it might be fifteen years before he would come to the use of a cane.

Before Gehrig came home from the Mayo Clinic, Eleanor went to their family physician, gave him the name of the disease and asked to be told the truth about it. The Doctor knew her well. He said quietly . . . "I think you can take it. And I think you should know."

Then he told her right between the eyes that

the disease was incurable and that her husband could not live more than two years.

Eleanor went home. She closed her door upon herself, shutting out the world. But before she could give in to grief and shock for the first and last time, she made a telephone call. It was to the Mayo Clinic. She had but one question to ask of the doctor there . . . "Have you told my husband?"

There is a rule or an understanding at the famous Clinic that patients are advised as to the seriousness of their condition. But in the short time that he had been at the hospital, Gehrig had captivated the staff. They had not the heart to tell him the truth and they so advised Eleanor Gehrig.

She begged . . . "Please promise me that you never will. Don't ever let him know. I don't want him to find out."

They promised.

Then only did Eleanor permit herself to weep.

The time of weeping was short. Lou came

home. He came home full of smiles and jokes, and the girl who met him was smiling and laughing too, though neither noticed that in the laughter of the other there was something a little feverish. They were too busy to notice. Too busy with their magnificent and gallant deception of one another.

Lou's cheer was based, outwardly, on the fact that he hadn't been an aging ball player, but that his sudden disintegration had been caused by the disease instead, a disease of which he promised Eleanor he would be cured before he learned to pronounce it.

And Eleanor, her heart breaking within her, chose to see his enforced layoff from baseball as an opportunity for another honeymoon, the chance to be together again.

The doctors said . . . "No baseball. Take things easy. You have a 50–50 chance to recover completely. It is not contagious. And there is no danger that your mind will be affected."

This was the basis of their intercourse, the

common meeting point of their outwardly expressed beliefs. Eleanor knew the truth and fought a constant fight of great valiance and intelligence to keep it from Lou. She had to be on the spot always to answer the telephone, to watch over him that people did not get to him, to look after the mail before he saw it. Ever present, menacing her was the one crackpot who might slip through the shields of love she placed about him, and tell him to his face that his case was hopeless.

15

AS TO what Lou knew—he never told anybody.

To all intents and purposes, he went into
the battle with his chin up and his determination blazing. He had overcome many ob-
stacles through life, poverty in his youth,
clumsiness in his profession, loneliness in his
relationship with other human beings. He
had taken a life that might have been a very
ordinary one, and by dint of persistency, ambition, courage and a beautiful cleanliness of
mind, had made something splendid and admired out of it. Now the life stuff itself was
attacked. He fought back as he had always
fought.

But this was one fight in which the knowledge was clear within him that the cards were stacked against him and that he would not win. He fought nevertheless. And we know the reason why. It was to keep up Eleanor's courage, to prevent her from realizing the hopelessness of his situation. He believed that she did not know the truth.

Gehrig continued to travel with the team for a time. As captain, he appeared at the start of each game and handed the line-up to the umpire, and then retired to the dugout. In every city on the circuit, the fans gave him an ovation when he appeared. The voice and the heart of the people were beginning to make themselves heard and felt.

His modesty could not bear the fuss and the public sympathy. He withdrew from handing the line-up to the umpire and appeared on the field no more.

On July 4th, 1939, there took place the most tragic and touching scene ever enacted on a baseball diamond—the funeral services for Louis Henry Gehrig.

Lou Gehrig attended them in person.

Gehrig Day, as it was called, was a gesture of love and appreciation on the part of everyone concerned, a spontaneous reaching out to a man who had been good and kind and decent, to thank him for having been so.

It was a day of sparkling sunshine and cheers, bunting and bands, a great and warm hearted crowd, fine gifts and fine speeches.

But only much, much later, seen in complete and true perspective do we feel the full and bitter impact of its tragic implications.

The suggestion that there be a Gehrig Appreciation Day began in the sports column of Bill Corum, who credits the idea to the telephone call of one Bill Hirsch.

The Journal took up the idea. Other columnists concurred. It was suggested that the All Star game be the occasion. But the Yankee management—or rather, Ed Barrow, a burly bear of a man with the kindest of hearts, did not want to share Gehrig's due with any other event. Gehrig Appreciation Day was set to take place between games of a Fourth of July double header.

The most touching conception of the day was the coming from the ends of the country of Gehrig's former team mates, the famous Murderer's Row, the powerful Yankees of 1927.

Bob Meusel, balding Benny Bengough, Gehrig's first pal, gray-eyed Mark Koenig, and dead-panned Poosh-'em-op Tony Lazzeri, the clown of the team, tall skinny Joe Dugan, and even skinnier and taller Pipp the Pickler, the Yankee first baseman whose place Gehrig had taken so many years ago, all came.

Little Everett Scott turned up, the man whose endurance record Gehrig had conquered so decisively, and the great pitching staff of yesterdays, Herb Pennock, from his Pennsylvania fox farm, Waite Hoyt from the broadcasting booths. George Pipgras was there too, but wearing the blue uniform of an umpire. Earl Combs and Art Fletcher still were in Yankee uniforms as coaches.

And finally there was George Herman Ruth. The Babe and Lou hadn't got along very well the last years they played together. Baseball writers knew that they weren't speaking. And after Babe had retired he had criticized Lou's long playing record in a newspaper interview. The original feud was a childish affair which began before Lou's marriage, women instigated, and which gains nothing in dignity or sense in re-telling. Suffice it to say that the Babe was there on that Requiem Day, with an arm around Lou and a whispered pleasantry that came at a time when Gehrig was very near to collapse from the emotions that turmoiled within him. It needed Babe's Rabelasian nonsense to make him smile.

Present too were Lou's more recent team

mates, the Bronx Bombers under Joe McCarthy, and the Washington Senators who were the opponents of the Yankees for the Fourth of July double header.

Sid Mercer, president of the Baseball Writers Association, was the master of ceremonies.

The principal speakers were Jim Farley, Postmaster General, and Mayor Fiorello La-Guardia. Sixty-one thousand, eight hundred and eight were in the stands. It was what was known as a Great Day.

To Lou Gehrig, it was goodbye to everything that he had known and loved.

It was goodbye to baseball, to the big steel and concrete stadium where he had served so long, to the neat green diamond with the smooth dirt paths cut by the sharp steel baseball cleats, to the towering stands with the waving pennons, the crowds, their roar and their color.

Goodbye too, to his colleagues, the friends

and the men with whom he had played for fourteen years, the happy, friendly men who had been his shipmates through life.

In the stands was all that he held dear, his family, mother and father seated in a box, unaware of his doom, his wife seated in another. Lifelong friends were in the boxes, cheering and applauding. And as Lou looked out over them gathered there in his honor, he knew he was seeing them thus for the last time.

For he was the living dead, and this was his funeral.

Gifts piled up for him, a silver service, smoking sets, writing sets, fishing tackle. They were from the Yankees, from his great rivals, the Giants, from the baseball writers and even from the ushers in the stadium and the peanut boys. The objects were a mockery, because he could no longer possess them. But the warmth of the feeling that prompted their purchase and presentation, melted the iron reserve in him and broke him down.

It was so human, so great, so heroic that he should have wept there in public before the sixty-eight odd thousand, not for pity of his situation, or for the beauty and sweetness of the world he would soon depart, but because the boy who all his life had convinced himself that he had no worth, that he did not matter and never would, understood on this day, for the first time perhaps, how much people loved him.

Not only his immediate family and his adored wife, his personal friends and acquaintances, but huge masses of plain, simple people, ordinary human beings with whom he felt a deep kinship, were broadcasting their warmth to him, sending it out through the air to the figure on the field below them. He was the lone receiving station. To tune in suddenly upon so much love was nearly too much for him.

The speeches were ended at last, the gifts

given, and the stadium rocked as wave after wave of cheers rolled down from the stands, huge combers of sound, and broke over him. For a little while as he stood at the microphones of the sound cameras and broadcasting companies, it seemed as though they might engulf him. He stood with his head bowed to the tumult—the tumult within and without, and pressed a handkerchief to his eyes to hold back the tears.

But when at last, encouraged by his friend Ed Barrow, he faced the instruments and the people behind them, the noise stopped abruptly. The echo barked once and was silent too. Everyone waited for what he would say. With a curled finger he dashed the tears that would not stay back from his eyes, lifted his head and brought his obsequies to the heart-breaking, never-to-be-forgotten finish, when he spoke his epitaph. . . .

"For the past two weeks you have been reading about a bad break I got. Yet today, I consider myself the luckiest man on the face of the earth. . . ."

The clangy, iron echo of the Yankee stadium, picked up the sentence that poured from the loud speakers and hurled it forth into the world. . . . "The luckiest man on the face of the earth . . . luckiest man on the face of the earth . . . luckiest man . . ."

16

PASS TO VALHALLA

THERE is an epilogue, because although the tale of Lou Gehrig—American Hero, really ended above, he lived for quite a while longer, and perhaps the simple story of how he lived what time was left to him and what he did, is the most heroic deed of all, the bravest, most gallant and most self-sacrificing.

For life is not the work of a master dramatist. The hero does not vanish in a cloud of fire at the supreme moment. No, life must be lived on until the curtain falls of its own accord, and that calls for the greatest heroism of all . . . the little things, the breaking smile, the cheery word, the laugh that covers pain, the light phrase that denies hopelessness and a sinking heart.

Almost two more years had to pass before the end came to Henry Louis Gehrig, and Eleanor says that during that time he was always gay and always laughing, cheerful, interested in everything, impatient only of unasked-for sympathy . . . in short he lived his daily life.

But he did more. And here we come to the final bit of heroism. With his doom sealed and his parting from the woman who had given him the only real happiness he had ever known, inevitable, he chose to spend his last days, not in one final feverish attempt to suck from life in two years all that he might have had in forty, but in work and service.

Mayor LaGuardia appointed him a City Parole Commissioner. The appointment was for a term of ten years, and one wonders whether the kindly Mayor did not know too of Gehrig's short remaining shrift on earth, and made the long term to encourage him.

And so for the next months, as long as he

was able to walk even with the assistance of others, Gehrig went daily to his office and did his work. He listened to cases, he studied them, he brought to it his thoroughness and his innate kindness and understanding.

He sat at his desk, even when no longer able to move his arms. When he wanted a cigarette, his wife or his secretary lit it for him and put it between his lips, removed it to shake the ash, replaced it again.

He listened to thief, vagabond, narcotic addict, pimp and prostitute. When there was help to be given, he gave it unstintingly of what strength there was left to him. He would not give in. He would not give up. He did not give up.

On June 2, 1941, Lou Gehrig died in the arms of his wife in their home in Larchmont.

But the final beauty of his story is that in a way, the tenacious man who had overcome every obstacle that ever faced him, overcame that last one too.

As close as one may come to attaining immortality in the hearts and minds of men, Gehrig achieved the life everlasting in that he left behind a vital part of himself. Men have tried to express it in the perpetuating of his playing number "4" and his locker in the Yankee Stadium, in the renaming of Concourse Plaza—"Gehrig Plaza," in the dedication of the late World Series to him, in the screening by Samuel Goldwyn of a picture, patterned after his life.

But the light that really shines like a friendly, beckoning beacon, is that of the spirit of a clean, honest, decent, kindly fellow gleaming through the gloom and darkness of a dispirited, disillusioned world.

It is less the man our weary souls have canonized, so much as the things for which he stood for and by which he lived and died. And for the seeing of those, we must all of us, great and small, be very grateful.

Baseball's Most Interesting Statistics

Compiled Through the Courtesy of
THE SPORTING NEWS

WORLD'S SERIES RESULTS
1903 to 1925, Inclusive

1903—Boston, A. L., 5 games; Pittsburgh, N. L., 3 games.

1904—No series.

1905—New York, N. L., 4 games; Philadelphia, A. L., 1 game.

1906—Chicago, A. L., 4 games; Chicago, N. L., 2 games.

1907—Chicago, N. L., 4 games; Detroit, A. L., 0 game; 1 tie.

1908—Chicago, N. L., 4 games; Detroit, A. L., 1 game.

1909—Pittsburgh, N. L., 4 games; Detroit, A. L., 3 games.

1910—Philadelphia, A. L., 4 games; Chicago, N. L., 1 game.

1911—Philadelphia, A. L., 4 games; New York, N. L., 2 games.

1912—Boston, A. L., 4 games; New York, N. L., 3 games; 1 tie.

1913—Philadelphia, A. L., 4 games; New York, N. L., 1 game.

1914—Boston, N. L., 4 games; Philadelphia, A. L., 0 game.

1915—Boston, A. L., 4 games; Philadelphia, N. L., 1 game.

1916—Boston, A. L., 4 games; Brooklyn, N. L., 1 game.

1917—Chicago, A. L., 4 games; New York, N. L., 2 games.

1918—Boston, A. L., 4 games; Chicago, N. L., 2 games.

1919—Cincinnati, N. L., 5 games; Chicago, A. L., 3 games.

1920—Cleveland, A. L., 5 games; Brooklyn, N. L., 2 games.

1921—New York, N. L., 5 games; New York, A. L., 3 games.

1922—New York, N. L., 4 games; New York, A. L., 0 game; 1 tie.

1923—New York, A. L., 4 games; New York, N. L., 2 games.

1924—Washington, A. L., 4 games; New York, N. L., 3 games.

1925—Pittsburgh, N. L., 4 games; Washington, A. L., 3 games.

WORLD'S SERIES RESULTS—*Cont'd*
1926 to 1941, Inclusive

1926—St. Louis, N. L., 4 games; New York, A. L., 3 games.

1927—New York, A. L., 4 games; Pittsburgh, N. L., 0 game.

1928—New York, A. L., 4 games; St. Louis, N. L., 0 game.

1929—Philadelphia, A. L., 4 games; Chicago, N. L., 1 game.

1930—Philadelphia, A. L., 4 games; St. Louis, N. L., 2 games.

1931—St. Louis, N. L., 4 games; Philadelphia, A. L., 3 games.

1932—New York, A. L., 4 games; Chicago, N. L., 0 game.

1933—New York, N. L., 4 games; Washington, A. L., 1 game.

1934—St. Louis, N. L., 4 games; Detroit, A. L., 3 games.

1935—Detroit, A. L., 4 games; Chicago, N. L., 2 games.

1936—New York, A. L., 4 games; New York, N. L., 2 games.

1937—New York, A. L., 4 games; New York, N. L., 1 game.

1938—New York, A. L., 4 games; Chicago, N. L., 0 game.

1939—New York, A. L., 4 games; Cincinnati, N. L., 0 game.

1940—Cincinnati, N. L., 4 games; Detroit, A. L., 3 games.

1941—New York, A. L., 4 games; Brooklyn, N. L., 1 game.

PENNANT WINNERS, AMERICAN LEAGUE

1901 to 1923, Inclusive

Year.	Club.	Manager.	Won	Lost	Pct.
1901—Chicago	Clark Griffith	83	53	.610
1902—Philadelphia	Connie Mack	83	53	.610
1903—Boston	James Collins	91	47	.659
1904—Boston	James Collins	95	59	.617
1905—Philadelphia	Connie Mack	92	56	.622
1906—Chicago	Fielder Jones	93	58	.616
1907—Detroit	Hugh Jennings	92	58	.613
1908—Detroit	Hugh Jennings	90	63	.588
1909—Detroit	Hugh Jennings	98	54	.645
1910—Philadelphia	Connie Mack	102	48	.680
1911—Philadelphia	Connie Mack	101	50	.669
1912—Boston	Garland Stahl	105	47	.691
1913—Philadelphia	Connie Mack	96	57	.627
1914—Philadelphia	Connie Mack	99	53	.651
1915—Boston	William Carrigan	101	50	.669
1916—Boston	William Carrigan	91	63	.591
1917—Chicago	Clarence Rowland	100	54	.649
1918—Boston	Edward Barrow	75	51	.595
1919—Chicago	William Gleason	88	52	.629
1920—Cleveland	Tris Speaker	98	56	.636
1921—New York	Miller Huggins	98	55	.641
1922—New York	Miller Huggins	94	60	.610
1923—New York	Miller Huggins	98	54	.645

PENNANT WINNERS, AMERICAN LEAGUE—*Continued*

1924 to 1941, Inclusive

Year.	Club.	Manager.	Won	Lost	Pct.
1924—Washington	Stanley Harris	92	62	.597
1925—Washington	Stanley Harris	96	55	.636
1926—New York	Miller Huggins	91	63	.591
1927—New York	Miller Huggins	110	44	.714
1928—New York	Miller Huggins	101	53	.656
1929—Philadelphia	Connie Mack	104	46	.693
1930—Philadelphia	Connie Mack	102	52	.662
1931—Philadelphia	Connie Mack	107	45	.704
1932—New York	Joseph McCarthy	107	47	.695
1933—Washington	Joseph Cronin	99	53	.651
1934—Detroit	Gordon Cochrane	101	53	.656
1935—Detroit	Gordon Cochrane	93	58	.616
1936—New York	Joseph McCarthy	102	51	.667
1937—New York	Joseph McCarthy	102	52	.662
1938—New York	Joseph McCarthy	99	53	.651
1939—New York	Joseph McCarthy	106	45	.702
1940—Detroit	Del Baker	90	64	.584
1941—New York	Joseph McCarthy	101	53	.656

PENNANT WINNERS, NATIONAL LEAGUE

1900 to 1922, Inclusive

Year.	Club.	Manager.	Won	Lost	Pct.
1900—Brooklyn		Edward Hanlon	82	54	.603
1901—Pittsburgh		Fred Clarke	90	49	.647
1902—Pittsburgh		Fred Clarke	103	36	.741
1903—Pittsburgh		Fred Clarke	91	49	.650
1904—New York		John McGraw	106	47	.693
1905—New York		John McGraw	105	48	.686
1906—Chicago		Frank Chance	116	36	.763
1907—Chicago		Frank Chance	107	45	.704
1908—Chicago		Frank Chance	99	55	.643
1909—Pittsburgh		Fred Clarke	110	42	.724
1910—Chicago		Frank Chance	104	50	.675
1911—New York		John McGraw	99	54	.647
1912—New York		John McGraw	103	48	.682
1913—New York		John McGraw	101	51	.664
1914—Boston		George Stallings	94	59	.614
1915—Philadelphia		Patrick Moran	90	62	.592
1916—Brooklyn		Wilbert Robinson	94	60	.610
1917—New York		John McGraw	98	56	.636
1918—Chicago		Fred Mitchell	84	45	.651
1919—Cincinnati		Patrick Moran	96	44	.686
1920—Brooklyn		Wilbert Robinson	93	61	.604
1921—New York		John McGraw	94	59	.614
1922—New York		John McGraw	93	61	.604

PENNANT WINNERS, NATIONAL LEAGUE—*Continued*

1923 to 1941, Inclusive

Year.	Club.	Manager.	Won	Lost	Pct.
1923—New York		John McGraw	95	58	.621
1924—New York		John McGraw	93	60	.608
1925—Pittsburgh		William McKechnie	95	58	.621
1926—St. Louis		Rogers Hornsby	89	65	.578
1927—Pittsburgh		Donie Bush	94	60	.610
1928—St. Louis		William McKechnie	95	59	.617
1929—Chicago		Joseph McCarthy	98	54	.645
1930—St. Louis		Charles Street	92	62	.597
1931—St. Louis		Charles Street	101	53	.656
1932—Chicago		R. Hornsby-C. Grimm	90	64	.584
1933—New York		William Terry	91	61	.599
1934—St. Louis		Frank Frisch	95	58	.621
1935—Chicago		Charles Grimm	100	54	.649
1936—New York		William Terry	92	62	.597
1937—New York		William Terry	95	57	.625
1938—Chicago		C. Grimm-L. Hartnett	89	63	.586
1939—Cincinnati		William McKechnie	97	57	.630
1940—Cincinnati		William McKechnie	100	53	.654
1941—Brooklyn		Leo Durocher	100	54	.649

AMERICAN LEAGUE BATTING LEADERS
1901 to 1921, Inclusive

Year—Player. Club.	G.	AB.	R.	H.	2B.	3B.	HR.	TB.	Ave.
1901—Lajoie, Phila.	131	543	145	220	48	13	13	333	.405
1902—Delahanty, Wash.	123	474	103	178	41	15	10	279	.376
1903—Lajoie, Cleveland	126	488	90	173	40	13	7	260	.355
1904—Lajoie, Cleveland	140	554	92	211	50	14	5	304	.381
1905—Flick, Cleveland	131	496	71	152	29	19	4	231	.306
1906—Stone, St. Louis	154	581	91	208	24	19	6	288	.358
1907—Cobb, Detroit	150	605	97	212	29	15	5	286	.350
1908—Cobb, Detroit	150	581	88	188	36	20	4	276	.324
1909—Cobb, Detroit	156	573	116	216	33	10	9	296	.377
1910—Cobb, Detroit	140	509	106	196	36	13	8	282	.385
1911—Cobb, Detroit	146	591	147	248	47	24	8	367	.420
1912—Cobb, Detroit	140	553	119	227	30	23	7	324	.410
1913—Cobb, Detroit	122	428	70	167	18	16	4	229	.390
1914—Cobb, Detroit	97	345	69	127	22	11	2	177	.368
1915—Cobb, Detroit	156	563	144	208	31	13	3	274	.369
1916—Speaker, Cleveland	151	546	102	211	41	8	2	274	.386
1917—Cobb, Detroit	152	588	107	225	44	23	7	336	.383
1918—Cobb, Detroit	111	421	83	161	19	14	3	217	.382
1919—Cobb, Detroit	124	497	92	191	36	13	1	256	.384
1920—Sisler, St. Louis	154	631	137	257	49	18	19	399	.407
1921—Heilmann, Detroit	149	602	114	237	43	14	19	365	.394

AMERICAN LEAGUE BATTING LEADERS—Continued
1922 to 1941, Inclusive

Year—Player. Club.	G.	AB.	R.	H.	2B.	3B.	HR.	TB.	Ave.
1922—Sisler, St. Louis	142	586	134	246	42	18	8	348	.420
1923—Heilmann, Detroit	144	524	121	211	44	11	18	331	.403
1924—Ruth, New York	153	529	143	200	39	7	46	391	.378
1925—Heilmann, Detroit	150	573	97	225	40	11	13	326	.393
1926—Manush, Detroit	136	498	95	188	35	8	14	281	.378
1927—Heilmann, Detroit	141	505	106	201	50	9	14	311	.398
1928—Goslin, Washington	135	456	80	173	36	10	17	280	.379
1929—Fonseca, Cleveland	148	566	97	209	44	15	6	301	.369
1930—Simmons, Phila.	138	554	152	211	41	16	36	392	.381
1931—Simmons, Phila.	128	513	105	200	37	13	22	329	.390
1932—Alexander, Det.-Bos.	124	392	58	144	27	3	8	201	.367
1933—Foxx, Philadelphia	149	573	125	204	37	9	48	403	.356
1934—Gehrig, New York	154	579	128	210	40	6	49	409	.363
1935—Myer, Washington	151	616	115	215	36	11	5	288	.349
1936—Appling, Chicago	138	526	111	204	31	7	6	267	.388
1937—Gehringer, Detroit	144	564	133	209	40	1	14	293	.371
1938—Foxx, Boston	149	565	139	197	33	9	50	398	.349
1939—J. DiMaggio, N. Y.	120	462	108	176	32	6	30	310	.381
1940—J. DiMaggio, N. Y.	132	508	93	179	28	9	31	318	.352
1941—Ted Williams, Bos.	143	456	135	185	33	3	37	335	.406

NATIONAL LEAGUE BATTING LEADERS
1900 to 1920, Inclusive

Year—Player.	Club.	G.	AB.	R.	H.	2B.	3B.	HR.	TB.	Ave.
1900—Wagner,	Pitts.	134	528	107	201	45	22	4	302	.380
1901—Burkett,	St. Louis	142	597	139	228	21	17	10	313	.382
1902—Beaumont,	Pitts.	131	544	101	194	21	6	0	227	.357
1903—Wagner,	Pitts.	129	512	97	182	30	19	5	265	.355
1904—Wagner,	Pitts.	132	490	97	171	44	14	4	255	.349
1905—Seymour,	Cin.	149	581	95	219	40	21	8	325	.377
1906—Wagner,	Pitts.	140	516	103	175	38	9	2	237	.339
1907—Wagner,	Pitts.	142	515	98	180	38	14	6	264	.350
1908—Wagner,	Pitts.	151	568	100	201	39	19	10	308	.354
1909—Wagner,	Pitts.	137	495	92	168	39	10	5	242	.339
1910—S. Magee,	Phila.	154	519	110	172	39	17	6	263	.331
1911—Wagner,	Pitts.	130	473	87	158	23	16	9	240	.334
1912—Zimmerman,	Chi.	145	557	95	207	41	14	14	318	.372
1913—Daubert,	Brooklyn	139	508	76	178	17	7	2	215	.350
1914—Daubert,	Brooklyn	126	474	89	156	17	7	6	205	.329
1915—Doyle,	New York	150	591	86	189	40	10	4	261	.320
1916—Chase,	Cincinnati	142	542	66	184	29	12	4	249	.339
1917—Roush,	Cincinnati	136	522	82	178	19	14	4	237	.341
1918—Wheat,	Brooklyn	105	409	39	137	15	3	0	158	.335
1919—Roush,	Cincinnati	133	504	73	162	19	13	3	216	.321
1920—Hornsby,	St. Louis	149	589	96	218	44	20	9	329	.370

NATIONAL LEAGUE BATTING LEADERS—Continued
1921 to 1941, Inclusive

Year—Player.	Club.	G.	AB.	R.	H.	2B.	3B.	HR.	TB.	Ave.
1921—Hornsby, St. Louis		154	592	131	235	44	18	21	378	.397
1922—Hornsby, St. Louis		154	623	141	250	46	14	42	450	.401
1923—Hornsby, St. Louis		107	424	89	163	32	10	17	266	.384
1924—Hornsby, St. Louis		143	536	121	227	43	14	25	373	.424
1925—Hornsby, St. Louis		138	504	133	203	41	10	39	381	.403
1926—E. Hargrave, Cin.		105	326	42	115	22	8	6	171	.353
1927—P. Waner, Pitts.		155	623	113	237	40	17	9	338	.380
1928—Hornsby, Boston		140	486	99	188	42	7	21	307	.387
1929—O'Doul, Phila.		154	638	152	254	35	6	32	397	.398
1930—Terry, New York		154	633	139	254	39	15	23	392	.401
1931—Hafey, St. Louis		122	450	94	157	35	8	16	256	.349
1932—O'Doul, Brooklyn		148	595	120	219	32	8	21	330	.368
1933—Klein, Philadelphia		152	606	101	223	44	7	28	365	.368
1934—P. Waner, Pitts.		146	599	122	217	32	16	14	323	.362
1935—Vaughan, Pitts.		137	499	108	192	34	10	19	303	.385
1936—P. Waner, Pitts.		148	585	107	218	53	9	5	304	.373
1937—Medwick, St. Louis		156	633	111	237	56	10	31	406	.374
1938—Lombardi, Cin.		129	489	60	167	30	1	19	256	.342
1939—Mize, St. Louis		153	564	104	197	44	14	28	353	.349
1940—Garms, Pittsburgh		103	358	76	127	23	7	5	179	.355
1941—Reiser, Brooklyn		137	536	117	184	39	17	14	299	.343

AMERICAN LEAGUE HOME RUN LEADERS

1900 to 1921, Inclusive

1900—(Not classed as major)
1901—Lajoie, Philadelphia.................... 13
1902—Seybold, Philadelphia.................... 16
1903—Freeman, Boston....................... 13
1904—H. Davis, Philadelphia.................. 10
1905—H. Davis, Philadelphia.................. 8
1906—H. Davis, Philadelphia.................. 12
1907—H. Davis, Philadelphia.................. 8
1908—Crawford, Detroit...................... 7
1909—Cobb, Detroit.......................... 9
1910—J. G. Stahl, Boston..................... 10
1911—Baker, Philadelphia.................... 9
1912—Baker, Philadelphia.................... 10
1913—Baker, Philadelphia.................... 12
1914—Baker, Philadelphia.................... 8
      Crawford, Detroit...................... 8
1915—Roth, Chicago-Cleveland............... 7
1916—Pipp, New York........................ 12
1917—Pipp, New York........................ 9
1918—Ruth, Boston........................... 11
      C. Walker, Philadelphia................. 11
1919—Ruth, Boston........................... 29
1920—Ruth, New York........................ 54
1921—Ruth, New York........................ 59

AMERICAN LEAGUE HOME RUN LEADERS—*Continued*

1922 to 1941, Inclusive

1922—K. Williams, St. Louis	39
1923—Ruth, New York	41
1924—Ruth, New York	46
1925—R. Meusel, New York	33
1926—Ruth, New York	47
1927—Ruth, New York	60
1928—Ruth, New York	54
1929—Ruth, New York	46
1930—Ruth, New York	49
1931—Ruth, New York	46
Gehrig, New York	46
1932—Foxx, Philadelphia	58
1933—Foxx, Philadelphia	48
1934—Gehrig, New York	49
1935—Foxx, Philadelphia	36
Greenberg, Detroit	36
1936—Gehrig, New York	49
1937—J. DiMaggio, New York	46
1938—Greenberg, Detroit	58
1939—Foxx, Boston	35
1940—Greenberg, Detroit	41
1941—Williams, Boston	37

NATIONAL LEAGUE HOME RUN LEADERS

1900 to 1921, Inclusive

1900—H. Long, Boston	12
1901—Crawford, Cincinnati	16
1902—Leach, Pittsburgh	6
1903—Sheckard, Brooklyn	9
1904—Lumley, Brooklyn	9
1905—Odwell, Cincinnati	9
1906—Jordan, Brooklyn	12
1907—Brain, Boston	10
1908—Jordan, Brooklyn	12
1909—Murray, New York	7
1910—Beck, Boston	10
Schulte, Chicago	10
1911—Schulte, Chicago	21
1912—Zimmerman, Chicago	14
1913—Cravath, Philadelphia	19
1914—Cravath, Philadelphia	19
1915—Cravath, Philadelphia	24
1916—D. Robertson, New York	12
F. Williams, Chicago	12
1917—D. Robertson, New York	12
Cravath, Philadelphia	12
1918—Cravath, Philadelphia	8
1919—Cravath, Philadelphia	12
1920—F. Williams, Philadelphia	15
1921—Kelly, New York	23

NATIONAL LEAGUE HOME RUN LEADERS—*Continued*
1922 to 1941; Inclusive

1922—Hornsby, St. Louis...................... 42
1923—F. Williams, Philadelphia................ 41
1924—Fournier, Brooklyn...................... 27
1925—Hornsby, St. Louis...................... 39
1926—L. Wilson, Chicago...................... 21
1927—L. Wilson, Chicago...................... 30
   F. Williams, Philadelphia............... 30
1928—L. Wilson, Chicago...................... 31
   Bottomley, St. Louis.................... 31
1929—Klein, Philadelphia..................... 43
1930—L. Wilson, Chicago...................... 56
1931—Klein, Philadelphia..................... 31
1932—Klein, Philadelphia..................... 38
   Ott, New York........................ 38
1933—Klein, Philadelphia..................... 28
1934—J. Collins, St. Louis.................... 35
   Ott, New York........................ 35
1935—Berger, Boston......................... 34
1936—Ott, New York......................... 33
1937—Ott, New York......................... 31
   Medwick, St. Louis.................... 31
1938—Ott, New York......................... 36
1939—Mize, St. Louis........................ 28
1940—Mize, St. Louis........................ 43
1941—Camilli, Brooklyn...................... 34

LEADING PITCHERS, AMERICAN LEAGUE

1901 to 1923, Inclusive

Year.	Pitcher.	Club.	Won	Lost	Pct.
1901—Clark Griffith		Chicago	24	7	.774
1902—Rube Waddell		Philadelphia	23	7	.767
1903—Earl Moore		Cleveland	22	7	.759
1904—Jack Chesbro		New York	41	12	.774
1905—Rube Waddell		Philadelphia	27	10	.730
1906—Edward Plank		Philadelphia	19	6	.760
1907—William Donovan		Detroit	25	4	.862
1908—Edward Walsh		Chicago	40	15	.727
1909—George Mullin		Detroit	29	8	.784
1910—Chief Bender		Philadelphia	23	5	.821
1911—Vean Gregg		Cleveland	23	7	.767
1912—Joseph Wood		Boston	34	5	.872
1913—Walter Johnson		Washington	36	7	.837
1914—Chief Bender		Philadelphia	17	3	.850
1915—Ernest Shore		Boston	19	7	.731
1916—Harry Coveleskie		Detroit	23	10	.697
1917—Carl Mays		Boston	22	9	.710
1918—Walter Johnson		Washington	23	13	.639
1919—Edward Cicotte		Chicago	28	7	.800
1920—James Bagby		Cleveland	31	12	.721
1921—Carl Mays		New York	27	9	.750
1922—Leslie (Joe) Bush		New York	26	7	.788
1923—Herbert Pennock		New York	19	6	.760

LEADING PITCHERS, AMERICAN LEAGUE—*Continued*

1924 to 1941, Inclusive

Year.	Pitcher.	Club.	Won	Lost	Pct.
1924—Walter Johnson		Washington	23	7	.767
1925—Stanley Coveleskie		Washington	20	5	.800
1926—George Uhle		Cleveland	27	11	.711
1927—Waite Hoyt		New York	22	7	.759
1928—Alvin Crowder		St. Louis	21	5	.808
1929—Robert Grove		Philadelphia	20	6	.769
1930—Robert Grove		Philadelphia	28	5	.848
1931—Robert Grove		Philadelphia	31	4	.886
1932—John Allen		New York	17	4	.810
1933—Robert Grove		Philadelphia	24	8	.750
1934—Vernon Gomez		New York	26	5	.839
1935—Elden Auker		Detroit	18	7	.720
1936—Irving Hadley		New York	14	4	.778
1937—John Allen		Cleveland	15	1	.938
1938—Robert Grove		Boston	14	4	.778
1939—Robert Grove		Boston	15	4	.789
1940—Lyn Rowe		Detroit	16	3	.842
1941—Vernon Gomez		New York	15	5	.750

LEADING PITCHERS, NATIONAL LEAGUE

1900 to 1921, Inclusive

Year.	Pitcher.	Club.	Won	Lost	Pct.
1900—Joe McGinnity		Brooklyn	29	9	.763
1901—Jack Chesbro		Pittsburgh	21	10	.677
1902—Jack Chesbro		Pittsburgh	28	6	.824
1903—Sam Leever		Pittsburgh	25	7	.781
1904—Joe McGinnity		New York	35	8	.814
1905—Sam Leever		Pittsburgh	20	5	.800
1906—Ed Reulbach		Chicago	19	4	.826
1907—Mordecai Brown		Chicago	20	6	.769
1908—Ed Reulbach		Chicago	24	7	.774
1909—Christy Mathewson		New York	25	6	.806
Howard Camnitz		Pittsburgh	25	6	.806
1910—Leonard Cole		Chicago	20	4	.833
1911—Rube Marquard		New York	24	7	.774
1912—Claude Hendrix		Pittsburgh	24	9	.727
1913—Grover Alexander		Philadelphia	22	8	.733
1914—Bill James		Boston	26	7	.788
1915—Grover Alexander		Philadelphia	31	10	.756
1916—Tom Hughes		Boston	16	3	.842
1917—Ferd Schupp		New York	21	7	.750
1918—Claude Hendrix		Chicago	20	7	.741
1919—Walter Ruether		Cincinnati	19	6	.760
1920—Burleigh Grimes		Brooklyn	23	11	.676
1921—Arthur Nehf		New York	20	10	.667

LEADING PITCHERS, NATIONAL LEAGUE—*Continued*

1922 to 1941, Inclusive

Year.	*Pitcher.*	*Club.*	*Won*	*Lost*	*Pct.*
1922—Pete Donohue	Cincinnati	18	9	.667
1923—Adolfo Lupue	Cincinnati	27	8	.771
1924—Emil Yde	Pittsburgh	16	3	.842
1925—Dazzy Vance	Brooklyn	22	9	.710
1926—Ray Kremer	Pittsburgh	20	6	.769
1927—Jess Haines	St. Louis	24	10	.706
1928—Larry Benton	New York	25	9	.735
1929—Charles Root	Chicago	19	6	.760
1930—Fred Fitzsimmons	New York	19	7	.731
1931—Paul Derringer	St. Louis	18	8	.692
1932—Lon Warneke	Chicago	22	6	.786
1933—Bud Tinning	Chicago	13	6	.684
1934—Dizzy Dean	St. Louis	30	7	.811
1935—Bill Lee	Chicago	20	6	.769
1936—Carl Hubbell	New York	26	6	.813
1937—Carl Hubbell	New York	22	8	.733
1938—Bill Lee	Chicago	22	9	.710
1939—Paul Derringer	Cincinnati	25	7	.781
1940—Fred Fitzsimmons	Brooklyn	16	2	.889
1941—Elmer Riddle	Cincinnati	19	4	.826

BASEBALL QUIZ

(Answers on Page 185)

1. In what World Series did Babe Ruth make his final appearance?

2. Who were the players who formed the famous "Pretzel Battery"?

3. What player performed the first unassisted triple play in American League history?

4. How many times was Rogers Hornsby named "Most Valuable Player" in the National League?

5. What two cities have been in the National League continuously since the circuit was organized in 1876?

6. Who played third base for the Chicago Cubs during the Tinker-Evers-Chance era?

7. What was Ban Johnson's occupation before he became president of the Western League?

8. Who invented the catcher's mask?

9. What was Walter Johnson's best strikeout total for any single season?

[182]

10. What pitcher hurled three double-headers —and won all six games—in one month?

11. Who hit the first home run in a World Series regulated by the National Commission?

12. Who was the winning pitcher of the first All-Star game played?

13. How many times did Dizzy Dean win twenty or more games per season?

14. What first baseman played in one hundred and sixty-three straight games without an error?

15. What teams won the pennant in the single seasons that the Union Association and Players' League operated?

16. When did Bill McKechnie capture his first National League flag?

17. What former major league president was a United States Senator and Governor?

18. What is the record for most passed balls by a catcher in a game?

19. How many innings did the longest scoreless game go?

20. When was Municipal Stadium, Cleveland, opened?

21. When was the major league schedule first lengthened to one hundred and fifty-four games.

22. In what park was the 1934 All-Star game staged?

23. What player made the most pinch-hits during a season?

24. What was the longest game in American League history?

25. Did a pinch-hitter ever homer in a World Series?

26. What big league coach slammed four homers in a game?

27. What famous pitcher was known as "Old Hoss"?

28. What club made most extra-base hits in a game?

29. What outfielder made most putouts in a double-header?

30. Against what club was Lefty Grove most successful during his career in the American League?

31. What club scored the most runs on opening day of season?

32. What club used most players in a season?

ANSWERS TO BASEBALL QUIZ

1. 1932.
2. Theodore Breitenstein and Heinie Peitz.
3. Neal Ball, Cleveland, in 1909.
4. Twice—1925 and 1929.
5. Boston and Chicago.
6. Harry Steinfeldt.
7. Sports writer.
8. Fred W. Thayer.
9. 313—1910.
10. Iron-Man Joe McGinnity in August, 1903.
11. Joe Tinker, Chicago Nationals, 1908.
12. Vernon Gomez.
13. Four.
14. John P. (Stuffy) McInnis.
15. St. Louis, U. A.; Boston, P. L.
16. 1925, with Pittsburgh.
17. Morgan G. Bulkeley of Connecticut, first N. L. President.
18. 12—by Frank Gardner, Washington A. A., May 10, 1884.
19. 18—Detroit-Washington, July 16, 1909.
20. July 31, 1932.
21. 1898.
22. Polo Grounds, New York.
23. Sam Leslie, New York Giants, 22 in 1932.
24. 24 innings, Red Sox-Athletics, September 1, 1906.
25. Never.
26. Chuck Klein, Phils.
27. Charles Radbourne.
28. Chicago Cubs, 16, July 3, 1883.
29. Lloyd Waner, 18, June 26, 1935.
30. Detroit. Won 60, lost 19.
31. Cleveland, 21, April 14, 1925.
32. Philadelphia Athletics, 56, in 1915.

[185]